10 LAWS
OF
COMMITMENT

FROM THE

SERMON
ON THE MOUNT

JOE SEABORN

Contents

Our Will Lost in God's Will

Introduction

Commitment

Historians are already calling ours the generation of "portable loyalties." The operative word in contemporary culture is *currently*. "I *currently* work in a restaurant." "We *currently* attend Day Spring Church." "*Currently* we're living on the edge of town."

Many assumptions that used to sit like foundational rock beneath our culture are quaking. Take these, for instance:

- Family values are strong and enduring
- The better the education, the better the wages
- Children will be better off than their parents
- The Bible is the main source of our moral principles
- We will retire with a well-funded and secure pension

5

Mobile loyalties are cropping up everywhere:

- A father says, "We're going to be attending that church down the road for a while. Our children like that youth group."
- A fiancée sits next to her soon-to-be husband and blurts out, "We're going to try this marriage thing for a while to see if it lasts."
- A teenager shrugs off going to his job at the fast food joint with the words, "Let them fire me. I can get another job."

Shallow loyalties aren't limited to the marketplace and mall. Popular Christian literature is using a whole new set of terms to describe Christian commitment today: hit-and-miss believers, flit faith, fragment faith, compartmental Christianity. Over the past several decades, transition has been so much with us that people are often more committed to transition than they are to substance.

In Alvin Toffler's popular book *Future Shock*, Toffler suggests that modern people perceive their lives as a series of modules. He brilliantly describes how people pursue their lives in segments or stations and how they may do different things with completely different degrees of maturity.

He notes that one of the favorite words of our time is "journey." To Toffler's insightful mind, the journey is the line that connects all the modules and gives a sense of continuity to life.

Let me set out a series of statements that reflect the mindset of our times, especially as it relates to the Christian faith. See if you have observed a similar pattern in your own community.

1 Most people no longer live in the house where they were born, as was true for many of their parents and grandparents.

2 Being a Christian for most people today is a process and not an arrival. Very few people are willing to testify to a specific time and place, for example, when they were "filled with the Spirit."

3 The idea of a spiritual journey — the common parlance of Christian testimony today — connotes both successes and failures. Most Christians assume that their spiritual lives will be a zigzag of failure and victory.

4 The idea of "journey" helps people feel that their spiritual failures and sins are not all that significant and that God will work it all out in the end.

5 For most younger Christians, creeds are far less important than testimonies about one's faith walk.

A great many people today avoid testifying to some degree about crisis — whether of salvation or sanctification — because they sense that such a statement communicates stagnation as opposed to progress (journey).

There is no shortage of talk about commitment. But like other terms, "commitment" has been diluted by the behavior and beliefs of our age. Today it can mean everything from a full surrender to God to hoping that we finish our "To Do" list by evening.

Commitment entails two dimensions. It involves both the things and persons for whom we develop a deep loyalty and the things and behaviors for which we develop a deep revulsion. Both are necessary in order to cultivate a balance in our lives. Scott Stanley and Howard Markman flesh out the point:

> We view commitment as encompassing two related constructs: personal dedication and constraint commitment. Personal dedication refers to the desire of an individual to maintain or improve the quality of his or her relationship for the joint benefit of the participants. It is evidenced by a desire and associated behaviors not only to continue in the relationship, but also to improve it, to sacrifice for it, and to invest in it, to link personal goals to it, and to seek the partner's welfare, not simply one's own.
>
> In contrast, constraint commitment refers to forces that constrain individuals to maintain relationships regardless of their personal dedication to them. Constraints may arise from either external or internal pressures, and they favor relationship stability by making termination of a relationship more economically, socially, personally or psychologically costly.[1]

The people who listened to the original Sermon on the Mount were struggling with the same problems we face today. It was not difficult to get them interested in the message of the gospel. It was easy to draw a crowd. It was terribly difficult to sustain their interest.

While the loaves and fish were being multiplied,
While their family members were being healed,
When the way was easy and the path plain,
The followers were plentiful.
But by the time Christ got to the cross,
Not one person would openly declare their loyalty to Him.

At Jesus' arrest, His own disciples deserted Him. Of the two that followed Him to the court of the high priest, even Peter denied Him and fled into the dawn. Only one remained — at a distance — with the women at the Cross.

There is a frightening attrition rate today among those who make decisions for Christ. While there is an astonishing interest in spirituality in our time, there is slim to nil enthusiasm for the kinds of daily disciplines that shape our souls in the image of God. In fact, the only kind of spirituality that people religiously avoid is Christianity. Every other "ism" under the sun is paraded and praised. But if it were left to the popular press to promote solid Christian commitment, the faith would die out tomorrow.

Christian souvenirs today can be sold by the millions if they are wrapped in pretty packaging and labeled "crossover." When they lose their novelty, however, they have to be repackaged according to the latest marketing trends.

The Committed Person Sees . . .

. . . feeding the mind as more important than feeding the emotions.

. . . accumulating integrity as more important than indulging the flesh.

. . . celebrating solidarity with others as more important than parading one's self.

. . . maintaining a teachable spirit as more important than demanding rights.

We are inundated with what Gore Vidal has described as "today's passion for the immediate and the casual."[2] We live in a world with more frenzy than faith. We have lost the ability to sit in silence, to bathe ourselves in thought, to think through our actions and what they will say about who we are inside. But please note: this first sermon of Christ is a call to "being" as much as it is to "doing." The foundation of God's radical gospel lies in such priceless and yet inexpensive endeavors as worship and prayer, Scripture reading and sharing in the Communion.

In a word, The Sermon on the Mount is a call to Christian commitment — to a life that gathers all its energy from finding and following the lifestyle of Christ. The lessons for living which we can draw from this single sermon make all other sermons pale in comparison. Even a rapid run through three chapters of Matthew's gospel opens up a number of insights.

And that's only a handful out of the armload of insights which this Sermon highlights and reinforces.

Sunday school specialist Elmer Towns has discovered that the typical person today needs to make seven to eight commitments to Christ before their "accumulated commitment" equals what might have come in a single experience with God two generations ago.

In our day, people make commitments more gradually than at any other time in recent history. Pastors are frustrated by forms which ask them to report "conversions" and "sanctification" commitments. They may have seen a person visit the altar but the ensuing lifestyle causes them to wonder if the commitment really stuck. How should they report it?

That is only one symptom of the "gradual commitment" which is very much with us. We may fight it and refuse to allow for any commitments except the kind that we believe counts. But if we do, we will miss a great many people who are coming to Christ but who, because of the incremental nature of commitment in our day, are taking shorter steps toward God than we might wish. Many today are coming to Christ so slowly and so haltingly that many leaders give up on these believers before they can learn to walk in salvation with confidence.

We need to begin using a new set of terms to describe the kind of Christian commitment many sincere people are making in our day. Here are a few suggestions:

1 INCRE-MITTMENT

This word combines the two key terms that characterize much commitment in our time. It is "incremental" but "sincere" commitment.

2 COMMIT-POINTS

This term reinforces the fact that decisions, even though they come in smaller pieces, still need to be considered decision points. A person cannot come to Christ — no matter how gradually — without making intentional decisions to become a Christian; thus the word "point."

3 COMMIT-BITS

It is fair to say that many people today "compile a commitment." That requires more patience on the part of those who are praying and guiding them, but just because the step is small does not mean that it is not a step. There are fewer and fewer dramatic salvation experiences in our day. We need to adjust our thinking to accept the fact that less drama does not necessarily mean less depth. Whether quiet and reserved or cavalier and boisterous, any step toward God is welcomed by Him with prodigal joy.

For those of us who know Christ, it is an ideal time to share our own testimony with new inspiration. Testimonies are one of God's most valuable tools for bringing conviction of sin and a sense of need into the life of the unbeliever. In a time when commitment is largely in decline, it is all the more vital for those of us who know its value to exercise it publicly and openly, giving praise to a God who can save us and keep what we have committed to Him through thick and thin.

May we as Christians add this prayer to our testimony:

> *Let me be committed to my family — they are my fellow travelers on the way to God.*
> *Let me be committed to evangelism — it is the kingdom of God.*
> *Let me be committed to the church — it is the beachhead of God.*
> *Let me be committed to prayer — it is the path to God.*
> *Let me be committed to people — they are made in the image of God.*
> *Let me be committed to purity — it is the way to see God.*
> *Let me be committed to love — it is the heartbeat of God.*

Please park your mind for a few extra seconds at the next two sentences:

The word

COMMITMENT,

which is popularly used today,

has replaced an older term,

SURRENDER.

DID WE LOSE SOMETHING IN THE TRANSLATION?

Instead of lamenting what we cannot recall, let us renew our own passion for God. Let us find ways in the daily round of our lives to show what it means to live under the total lordship of Christ. In the end, it will be our own consistent and committed life which will challenge others around us to go deeper with God.

An Easy Forty Dollars

It was 4:30 on a Monday afternoon. Face lathered, I was standing in front of the bathroom mirror, prettying myself up before running off to do a fund-raiser for the local rescue mission.

My eight-year-old son Joseph, just in from playing ball, leaned against the door to catch his breath.

"Where are you going, Dad?" he asked.

"I'm going to help raise money for the rescue mission."

"What's a rescue mission?"

"Well, son," I answered, scraping lather from my face, "it's like a home for people who have no home. The people at the mission give homeless people food and a place to sleep while they are struggling to get along in life."

Joseph was quiet. His eyes panned the room, looking at nothing in particular. Then just as quietly as he had come, he was gone. As I shaved, I thought about his quiet spirit, his sensitive reflection.

A few seconds later, there he stood again, a ten-dollar bill in his hand.

"What's that for, son?"

"The rescue mission," he said in a serious tone. "Will you take it over there for me and give it to those people who have no home?"

I studied him for a moment. "But I thought you were saving that for baseball cards."

"Yeah, but I can wait. I want to give it to those men who don't have a home."

When I dropped his ten dollars in the offering plate, I remembered the widow and her two pennies.

By the time Joseph came home from school the next day, I had made another trip — to the baseball card store — bought a full box of 1996 Fleer Baseball cards. Easiest forty dollars I ever spent.

As you study these Ten Laws of Commitment from the Sermon on the Mount, ask God to take you to a whole new level of love and loyalty to His kingdom. As you hear the word of Christ echoing against the hillside overlooking the Sea of Galilee, allow Him to write His laws more deeply on the pulsing tables of your own heart.

Endnotes

[1]Scott Stanley and Howard J. Markman, "Assessing Commitment in Social Relationships," *Journal of Marriage and Family* 54 (August 1992): 598.

[2]Eugene Peterson, *A Long Obedience in the Same Direction* (Downers Grove: InterVarsity, 1980), p. 12.

Mind Movers

1 Do you believe that people a generation ago were more committed to Christ than Christians are today? How did our parents and grandparents express their allegiance to Christ differently from people today? Are there ways in which the present generation's commitment level has improved over commitment levels of the past?

2 If living for God is so good, why aren't more people doing it? Have you ever known a person who lived for God and then turned from Him? What might cause a person to do this?

3 Should pastors and teachers make the cause of Christ more demanding? Has the Christian faith been watered down so much that people are drawn to it because it's too easy? Does the cost of living for Christ vary from generation to generation?

4 Each generation will be remembered for being committed to something. What will that be for our generation? What were our priorities and commitments as a society?

5 As you think over the cast of characters in the Bible, what people stand out in your mind as great examples of commitment. What makes their commitment impressive to you?

Allegiance

I Pledge Allegiance to the Lamb

Cynthia Carter's picture sits on a prominent shelf in my office. It may be just another pretty face to a visitor, but it ministers to me. When I need power and perspective for the pressures I am facing, I turn to that picture. It reminds me that God's love has an amazing reach, and that God honors those who stand firm in His love.

Ten years ago Cynthia Carter was on the edge. When she had married Warren three years before, things were picture perfect. He held an engineering degree from Cornell and was already climbing the corporate ladder in fast-forward motion. Their first home was a dream house. There were banquets and parties and enough corporate perks to qualify them as world travelers. Church on Sunday, money on Monday, a baby on the way — it was cake with all the icing.

She was surprised one day to find an odd-smelling, talcum-like powder in Warren's shirt pocket. Why would he have talcum powder in his pocket? She had also noticed that he was spending ten and eleven hours a day in the office. When she added on two more hours for the trip back and forth, he was almost never home during daylight hours.

His parents from across the country began quizzing her about Warren's behavior. She tried to cover for him, but not for long. When the dream began to collapse, the fall was stunning. First the excessive working hours, then cocaine, then alcohol, then the abuse which nearly cost the baby's life. Cynthia was on the verge of suicide. Her own words summed up the tragedy.

"I felt like hell would be a relief. Anything to let me wake up from this nightmare." Cynthia had grown up with the deep belief that marriage is for keeps. Any less commitment and she would long since have bailed out.

Warren called his father. "Dad, Cynthia's leaving me. She says she can't take it anymore. What in the world can I do?"

Carl's answer surprised his son. "Warren, you're not going to believe me, but this very morning I begged God to bring you back to Him at any cost. Is this the cost?"

Warren was dazed. He got in his car and headed up a mountain to take his life. Too much. A child he had almost killed. A wife on the verge. His own life caught in the tangle of drugs and alcohol. This was no way to live. And certainly no way to die.

On his way up the mountain he saw a hand-painted sign on the side of the road, "CHRISTIAN MEN'S RETREAT — TURN HERE." To his own amazement, Warren turned.

Two days later he drove back down that same road a different man. His first words to his Dad were powerful: "Dad, this is your prodigal son, I'm on my way home." Three thousand miles away, Carl Price sat on the side of his bed and wept.

Cynthia could hardly believe it. Could it be real? A new husband, a new home? The roller coaster had run wild but was now moving smoothly on a new track.

That's why this picture sits on my desk. If ever there was a portrait of allegiance, Cynthia is it. If ever there was a picture of courage in the middle of calamity, it is the face of Cynthia Carter.

Oh, and one more thing. Did I mention that Cynthia is not the only one in the picture? To her left is Christopher, her healthy ten-year-old son. And to her right is Warren. The picture is their prayer card for missionary service. Today they lead a group of missionaries who are serving with International Missions Teams Russia.

Cynthia's loyalty paid off. It cost her initially, but the reward was worth the price. The gleam in her eye shows through even in this picture.

14

In His Sermon on the Mount, Christ calls us to stand and pledge allegiance to a holy lifestyle. A lifestyle like the one Cynthia lived out in a collapsing home. And the one she is now living out in Russia.

This call to allegiance is laid out in what we might call our CONTRACT WITH CHRISTIANITY:

1 I PLEDGE ALLEGIANCE TO A CHRISTLIKE SPIRIT.
(Matt. 5:1-10)

If you piece together the "blesseds" found here at the beginning of the sermon, they will form the face of Jesus. He is the living-color version of what these statements say in black and white. As God, Jesus couldn't really help it. He didn't need to. Other preachers shouldn't tell you to be like them, but Jesus could — and did. As one man said, "God doesn't sit around heaven contemplating Himself, but if He does, it's a worthwhile pastime."

The spirit He is calling us to is the spirit which He Himself carried around in His heart. Why would a person call himself Christian and not live the life? What would motivate such hypocrisy? Why claim the name and deny the lifestyle? That's not loyalty, that's a lie. A person who calls himself by the most lofty label ever applied to a human being should strive with every fiber to live up to the title. Just as ice is cold, water is wet and air is fluid. So the Christian should pass for a Christian by the simple criterion of common sense.

One of the greatest attractions in the Christian community is a thoroughly Christian life. Today the label "Christian" is easy to slap on your resume. A vague association with Christianity through a grandparent or a childhood Sunday school and we are ready to claim our Christian name. But the connection is about as dependable as a house of cards built on sand over a fault line.

Everybody looks good on paper. It's only as you meet people and know them and read their hearts that you discover the depth of their loyalty. Putting the title "Christian" on a resume doesn't make one a Christian any more than driving a tricycle into a garage makes it a car. The surest sign of a genuine faith is a Christlike attitude.

Carrying the name of "Christian" can be costly. As it should be. It ought to be saturated with ordeal, mellowed by sacrifice and matured by discipline. A Christian is a person who has risked everything in a divine game in which the only options are a deepening holiness or a deadly dry-rot.

When the going is tough and rough — when they drive nails through your hands and a spear through your side and fire a round of hate through your heart — when you stay steady in all that, you are moving closer to the core of the Christian faith.

15

One glance at a golden mature saint, whose life drips with the nectar of holiness, and you know the path to take. The disciple of Christ exudes a spirit of peace in the storm,

joy in the journey,

contentment in the chaos,

hope in a pipe dream world.

Theirs is not a creed followed by a cave, a facade hiding a vacuum. They have the goods. And they can exhibit these qualities because their loyalty is linked to a power beyond this life. They know that while they belong here, they also belong to a Kingdom not made with hands, eternal in the heavens.

A Christlike spirit will not lose. Nothing can ever defeat it. Eternity is stamped across the side, and God is holding the blotter.

2 I PLEDGE ALLEGIANCE TO MY ROLE IN THE KINGDOM OF GOD. (Matt. 5:13-16)

It is impossible to think of salt without thinking of its function, or to think about light without thinking of its benefits. It ought to be equally impossible to think of a Christian apart from his role in the shaping of the Kingdom. Salt must give its life to season. Light must leave its source to shine. A Christian must sacrifice himself without reservation in order to change the world.

It is often said that Boomers and Xers don't develop loyalty, they cultivate useful relationships and meaningful encounters.

There's a lot of the wrong number one rolled into that philosophy — a whole lot of selfishness going on. The Kingdom of God is not for the well-intentioned, but for the desperate. It requires us to line up forever behind a different Number One. Jesus says, "Seek first His Kingdom and His righteousness; and all these things shall be added to you" (Matt. 6:33 NASB).

We want to be associated with many causes but dedicated to none. That's not good. To try to be committed to every cause is to be committed to no cause at all.

A. W. Tozer's point should be painted on a poster and held up at the exit of every church door: "The world is not a playground, but a battleground. Go out and do battle for the kingdom that counts."

In order to fulfill God's role for us in the Kingdom, there are several valuable clues to keep in mind:

● **We find our truest purpose on earth when we actively promote the Kingdom of heaven.**

Our claim to be Christians must be backed up by our walk as witnesses. A clock must tick. An airplane must fly. A copier must make copies. And a Christian must duplicate Christ . . . As a keeper of the Kingdom.

- **We discover our true purpose only in relationship.**

Home-style worship is like wanting to be a soldier without joining the army. To use another metaphor, no piece of the puzzle is the whole picture by itself. Only as we find our right link with God and then with each other can we finally fulfill God's call upon our lives.

Look at the cross. There is an upright beam and a crossbeam. Think of the upright beam as your relationship with God and the crosspiece as your relationship with others. If you let your relationship with God falter and collapse, the rest of your relationships come tumbling down with it. At heart, all relational struggles we wrestle with on earth can best be repaired by first strengthening our relationship with our Father who is in heaven.

"Relationship with God, and Our Relationship with Others."

● **We find our role in the Kingdom by being the unique person God made us to be.**

Popularity is usually gotten at the price of being dull.

God made us like He made us, and He likes us like we are.

Too much comparison and competition takes place in the church today. So many people try so hard to be like other people that they wind up being neither themselves or anyone else.

The call of the Bible is to so identify with Christ that we increasingly become the normal person that we should be. That can only occur as we take out our hearts and hand them over to Jesus, then stand back and watch Him blend our unique gifts with the Kingdom's needs. The spirit of allegiance which Christ is seeking from us could be defined like this:

> "Loyalty includes fidelity in carrying out one's duties to the person or group of persons who are the object of loyalty; but it embraces more than that, for it implies an attitude, perhaps an affection or sentiment, toward such persons. Furthermore, at the very least, loyalty requires the complete subordination of one's own private interests in favor of giving what is due, and also the exclusion of other competing interests."[1]

Instead of *wondering* what might have been if you had been somebody else, begin *wandering* the possibilities of what will happen as you become more fully yourself.

I PLEDGE ALLEGIANCE TO THE TEN COMMANDMENTS. (Matt. 5:17-19); (Ex. 20:1-17)

There's a reason why God demands that we "love the Lord your God with all your heart" (Deut. 6:5). Loyalty starts in the heart. We will never do anything for long which we don't do from desire.

Love without law is a sloppy love. When Augustine said, "Love God and do as you please," he was saying that a 100% commitment to God will inspire you to do as He pleases and enjoy it. George Gritter lined it up with Ds: "A

duty which becomes a **desire** will ultimately become a **delight.**"

If the mere mention of the Ten Commandments sets off a negative reaction in our minds, we need to fall more deeply in love with their Author. When our love for God is radical, we look for ways to make Him happy. His "To-Do" List becomes our "Love List" — a litany of guidelines that we feel privileged to obey.

Eternal life is not just the fifth step after the four spiritual laws. Nor is it a special perk tacked on to the Ten Commandments. Eternal life is a joyful, stirring, happy thing, a way of living in which our behavior, our beliefs and our very being sing in harmony to the glory of God.

In our "menu mindset" world, too many want to look over the Ten Commandments to see which ones they like. But the Ten Commandments are not up for referendum. The sovereignty of God is not subject to a vote. The only proper way to approach this Decalogue of Life is to start out by assuming that if God said it, it can only help you. Then lock in to following the list to the letter.

> Frank O'Connor, the Irish writer tells in one of his books how as a boy, he and his friends would make their way across the countryside and when they came to an orchard wall that seemed too high and too doubtful to try and too difficult to permit their voyage to continue, they took off their hats and tossed them over the wall — and then they had no choice but to follow them.

With the Ten Commandments, you throw your heart over the wall. On the other side is life.

Jesus didn't toss a hat, He took up a cross. Now He calls us to also take up our crosses and head for the hill. A person who assumes the cross of Christ and heads in any other direction than Calvary is wasting his time. Calvary is the only place where crosses are planted. Simply put, Jesus bids us come and die.

4 I PLEDGE ALLEGIANCE TO THE HABITS OF HOLY LIVING. (Matt. 6:1-18)

Christianity is both a beginning point and a path. It is a start and a process. It is an action followed by habits which feed the conversion decision. "Prayer" and "fasting" are not decorations for the Christian life; they are its lifeline.

A few years ago I went through a time of inner spiritual struggle. I had been to college and seminary and had a head full of good ideas about God. But I was grappling with my own faith. Did God really exist? Was I holding onto a bubble which would burst at death? Or sooner?

Not right away, but somewhere in the process of that struggle, I made a commitment to God. I had always said that living the Christian life was worth it even if there were no heaven or hell. This period of intense doubt gave me a chance to test that belief. I committed myself to obeying the Word and will of God even though God seemed far, far away.

As I glance back with an eye toward analysis, I believe that my commitment to walk by faith without sight, to trust God even when I could not sense Him, may well have been one of the best learning curves of my spiritual life. Legend has it that when the Israelites came to cross the Red Sea, nothing happened until the first man stepped into the water.

In a world trapped in every habit under the sun, give us a generation of Christians who celebrate their bondage to Christ. When Bill Bright began the Campus Crusade movement, he took a vow to be a bond slave of Christ. It paid off. Richly!

Here's the irony. Sinful habits are enslaving; holy habits are freeing. Sinful habits take us farther and farther from our true selves. Holy habits help us to be increasingly normal — the way God planned us in the first place.

The prodigal son, indulging in the habits of the hogpen, was a long way from home. But he was also a long way from himself. That's why a packed little phrase explodes from the text like a firecracker: "But when he came to himself, he said, 'How many of my father's hired servants have bread enough to spare, and I perish with hunger! I will arise and go to my father. . . .'" (Luke 15:17-18 NKJV). Good move. But he also went home to himself.

I'm a long way from the holy lifestyle I'd like to live, but I crave the ideal. You may have to look for me in the nurseries of heaven someday, but at least I will have made it. I have discovered that God is not so much interested in getting us somewhere as He is in making something of us along the way.

Here are a few habits you'll never need to kick:

INGESTING THE TRUTH. (Phil. 4:6)

Feed on Him in your heart with thanksgiving.

The same lips that call us to search the Scriptures also call us to consider the lilies. The Bible and the fields all harmonize in their witness to the Father's goodness and eternal love.

bINHALING THE SPIRIT. (John 20:22)

He breathed upon them and said, "Receive the Holy Spirit." Let your natural breathing be a personal parable of the inbreathing of the Holy Spirit.

cENJOYING THE FELLOWSHIP. (Heb. 10:25)

Never neglect an opportunity to associate with other strength-givers. Those folks who used to testify that they were there "every time the doors were open" may have found a secret worth sharing.

dENRICHING THE WORLD. (Mark 6:37)

When Jesus told His disciples, "You give them something to eat," He knew we would see that command as referring to more than loaves and fishes.

Never let it be said of you that you . . .

cared, but only minimally
gave, but only miserly
lived, but only meagerly
walked, but only haltingly
sowed, but only sparingly
spoke, but only timidly
moved, but only aimlessly
fought, but only half-heartedly
planned, but only whimsically
mattered, but only marginally
loved, but only selfishly.

Purple Purgatory

Recently while my son was getting a haircut at a local salon, I decided to check out the tanning beds. I had seen them advertised in the paper and had a rush of curiosity about how they actually worked. The attendant told me the first 15 minutes were free anyway, so I agreed to try one out. The lady guided me into the room, pointed to a set of instructions posted on the wall, and closed the door.

A surge of guilt swept over me. I still don't know why. I had grown up playing in the sun so it wasn't the tanning factor. It was only 15 minutes, so surely I wouldn't experience "human meltdown." But I still felt guilty.

I finally figured it must be a modesty thing. To get the full body tan, you had to disrobe and I simply couldn't bring myself to do that in a public place. Somebody might walk in — somebody with an appointment — and chase me out half dressed. So I did the wise thing. I took off my shoes and eased onto the tanning bed fully clothed! Socks, pants, belt, shirt, tie, just like you'd need in a casket. When I flicked the switch, I had the same fear you'd get by tinkering with a time bomb.

For nearly five minutes I lay there worrying about who might burst through the door and see me. I could lose my job for this kind of nonsense. And even if I did get a tan, how would I explain how it happened? It was a torture chamber. Purple purgatory. After what felt like a week, I flicked the X-ray off and eased back into my shoes — with ten full minutes to spare! To my relief, when I glanced in the mirror I was as white as a sheet.

The lady at the desk told me the monthly rates were listed in the basement. I assured her that I had just enjoyed — strike that — endured my first and last tanning bed. The next time I plan to lay in a position like that somebody else will be in charge of the arrangements.

A great many people enter into their Christian faith with a healthy dose of hesitation. They may have seen a few hypocrites and wonder if this Christian thing will really work. Others have never deeply committed themselves to anything and feel that something the size of eternity shouldn't be rushed into headlong. But those of us who have tried Him have found that God never does anything to us but make us better. The more you give, the better you live.

The Ultimate Act of Allegiance

One of the men sitting on the hill and listening to the Sermon on the Mount that afternoon was a fisherman who would later give his life for the cause.

The *Acts of Peter*, a book written during the early days of the church but not included in our Bible, tells of Peter on his way to Rome. There in Rome, because of his strong stand for God, Peter generated a new round of enemies. Simon Magus, an old nemesis first introduced to us in Acts, chapter eight, spread rumors about Peter and raised new ire.

But Peter would not be silent. His fiery devotion to Christ had been declared years before in the words, "We must obey God rather than men" (Acts 5:29 NASB). He was not about to change now.

We learn from the *Acts of Peter* that the Great Fisherman won four women to Christ right out of Agrippa's court. The outrage grew. Then Xanthippe, the wife of one of the emperor's friends, converted. A price was placed on Peter's head. Rightly fearing for his life, Peter's friends urged him to hurry out of the city and hide. The crisis swelled to the bursting point.

But as Peter fled the city of Rome, Christ met him on the road coming the other way. Peter looked at Him and spoke the words made famous in the movie of the same name, "Quo vadis, Domine?" (Where are you going, Lord?) Jesus replied, "I am going into the city to be crucified again."

"To be crucified again?" Peter expressed surprise. Then it dawned on him. Jesus was going into the city to be crucified on the very cross from which Peter was running away.

Peter turned back to die. In a cruel twist of destiny, Peter's wife was crucified before his eyes. His final words to her in that dreadful hour were brief and succinct, "Remember the Lord." His own desperate prayer years ago as he sank into the Sea of Galilee, had been just as brief: "Lord, save me!" (Matt. 14:30).

As Peter was led to his own crucifixion, he asked to be nailed to the cross upside down because he was not worthy to die in an upright position like his Lord. The soldiers granted his request. His allegiance in life became the ultimate act of allegiance in death.

You are not yet ready to live for God until you are willing to die for God. And that kind of allegiance is guaranteed to end finally in life.

Endnote

[1] R. E. Ewin, "Loyalty and Virtues," *Philosophical Quarterly* 42 (October 1992): 405.

Mind Movers

1 Why is there a crisis of commitment today?

2 Is there a connection between patriotism to a nation and loyalty to the Kingdom of God? If a person is critical of his country, can he be deeply devoted to God? Does being a Christian require that a person be either Republican or Democrat?

3 Are so many things clamoring for our attention today that we honestly can't be as deeply committed as we once were? Do we have a finite quantity of commitment or can commitment be increased?

4 What are occasions when the loyalty of a Christian to the Kingdom of God might conflict with commitments in other directions?

5 Is it possible to have intermittent loyalty? Does loyalty have to be sustained or is that frankly unrealistic in our time?

6 Read John 6:60-71. In this passage, what does Christ teach about loyalty to the Kingdom?

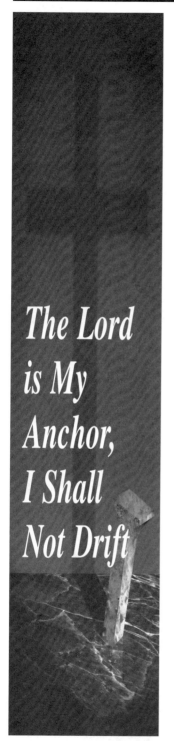

2

Conviction

The Lord is My Anchor, I Shall Not Drift

Teresa and Connie were stunned. They glanced at each other in disbelief. As quickly as she could, Connie braked and stared in the rearview mirror to double-check. Sure enough, a young woman in shirtsleeves was walking along a forsaken stretch of road. The temperature stood at minus ten degrees. The wind whipped it even lower. The woman wore no cap, no gloves, no scarf. And oddest of all, her coat was crumpled under her arm. What on earth was she doing?

They stopped and backed up. Connie yelled out the window, "Hey, can we help you?"

The young woman stepped toward them. "Yes, I'm freezing. My car stopped back down the road."

"Hop in quick." The lady opened the rear door and slid into the back seat.

"What are you doing carrying your coat in this weather? You could die."

The young woman nodded. She slipped the coat out from under her arm and unfolded it.

Inside lay her three-month-old baby. "I figured if one of us had to die, I wanted it to be me."

It's more than a parable for a winter's day. It's the spirit that Christ is calling for in Matthew 5:13-16. A resolve that puts the cause before the comfort. A decision that lines up our priorities in the divine order.

The Sermon on the Mount is known for housing the Beatitudes. Or as Robert Schuller calls them, "The 'Be' Attitudes." In order for conviction to mark our lives, this sermon also calls us to a set of "The 'Don't Be' Attitudes."

1 DON'T BE CONFORMED; BE THE CHANGE AGENT.
(Matt. 5:13-16)

There are two ways that salt can lose its saltiness. It can either sit idly on the shelf too long or give its strength to a helping of green beans. When sprinkled on the beans, it fulfills its purpose for being — changing its world by giving itself away.

New Testament Christians hazarded their lives for the gospel. With God's coaching, they turned their world upside down (Acts 17:6). Too many Christians today don't have enough conviction to tip over a Coke can, let alone the world.

There are five kinds of change agents in our communities:

Mind Movers. . . . . Gently, warmly, firmly winning others over to the mind of Christ.

Process Helpers . . . . Helping others arrive at a strategy for moving from vague to clear Christian values.

Care Givers . . . . Offering hope and healing to those whose values and ensuing habits of living have caused them pain and suffering.

Resource Linkers . . . . Creating a network of resources and people who can support a needy person on the way to Christlikeness.

Confidence Builders. . . . . . . Being there at regular intervals along the way to share a word of hope and a hug of encouragement.

There are several clear-as-crystal characteristics of a person of conviction, a person who stands firm in a freefall world. Soak each one of these for its full flavor.

- *A person of conviction has a good reason for why he stands his ground.*
- *A person of conviction is not ashamed to declare his faith everywhere.*
- *A person of conviction has a maturing sense of his life's purpose.*
- *A person of conviction gathers all his life around a single core of truth.*
- *A person of conviction lives on the offensive toward the world around him.*
- *A person of conviction knows that most of his lifetime won't be spent on this earth.*
- *A person of conviction fixes on his chosen destiny in spite of the detours.*

Archimedes, arguably the most inventive of the ancient Greek mathematicians, once said, "Give me a place to stand and I will move the earth." God has given us a place to stand. "Your word, O Lord, is eternal; it stands firm in the heavens" (Ps. 119:89 NIV). If we will stand on the Word, we too can move the earth. Never ask the size of the task; only ask the size of our God.

Don't glance at God and gaze at the Goliaths. Glance at the Goliaths and gaze at God. David did, and he only needed one of the five smooth stones.

2 DON'T BE TIMID; STAND YOUR GROUND (Matt. 7:24-27)

The Founder of our faith was a simple God-intoxicated man. He knew there were critics in the crowd that day on the hillside. In Jerusalem the critics were even thicker. If he had been up for a pastoral vote, a good number of those who heard his trial sermon would have voted "no."

Martin Luther did not start a reformation with a pulse poll. He declared his position and nailed his beliefs to the most public door he could find. With the sizable weight of the official church bearing down on him, he spoke his heart, "Here I stand, God help me."

It is hard for God to use us while we are second-guessing ourselves. He cannot lodge His eternal truth in a heart that is shifting with the sands of change. Let's not fool ourselves. The advocates for total tolerance and democratic diversity are hypocrites at heart. When Christians take a clear stand for Christ and challenge an opposing view, the opponents bristle and dig in with the zeal of a badger. So much for their policy of openness.

But the gospel of Christ is still true whether people embrace it or not. You don't dethrone the Savior by thumbing your nose. Our God reigns. We can bank our faith on it. At the end of things, the kingdoms of this world will become the kingdoms of our God and of His Christ. We may as well go ahead and stake our claim in the Kingdom which will endure. When every other kingdom on earth lies in the dust bins of history, only one will remain.

The foundation of our faith is what gives us confidence, not the faith itself. Our foundation is far greater than our faith. One man laughed, "My hope is built on nothing less than Scofield's notes and Wesley Press." Pretty small base. If you have staked your claim with Christ, stand your ground. The earth may move on all four sides, but you are standing on the Rock of Ages. Stand firm.

> *Commitment is more like a stake than an anchor. You drag an anchor and it is still an anchor, but if you pull up a stake, it is just a stick.*

3 DON'T BE AMBIGUOUS; DECLARE YOURSELF CLEARLY. (Matt. 5:33-37)

There are only two types of people when it comes to expressing a view of life — those who hold a view and refuse to admit it; and those who hold a view and are happy to admit it. No person is neutral in this regard. The only difference is the degree to which we acknowledge our posture.

Sociologists are using the term "postmodernism" to describe the mindset of our age. In short, postmodernism holds that all roads must eventually lead to God because truth is never absolute. In such a tolerant climate, people are not penalized for being as irreverent as they once were. Instead, the criticism comes if you are a believer.

Religions like Islam and Hinduism are associated with ethnic populations and thus come under the constitutional protection of the "religions of diversity and tolerance" phrase. Oddly, Christianity is not associated with any particular population, so it is open to attack and even ban. Most people no longer assume they are governed by divine right. Christianity is far from being the Christendom it once was and is increasingly disdained.

Secularism has arisen as the religion of the masses with its shibboleths of:

> Politics without principle
> Wealth without work
> Pleasure without conscience
> Productivity without ethics
> Worship without sacrifice
> Science without God
> Knowledge without character

Pure neutrality is a myth. We Christians often hedge our words because we don't want to come off as too dogmatic in our pluralistic world. But let's set the record straight. As Christians we don't *have* to be right, all we desire is that we *are* right. If you stand for truth, you don't need to raise your voice.

All Roads lead to 'Roam.'

I wish you could have known Grady Kelly. A little hunchbacked, soaked in sainthood, he sat about five pews back. The last adjective you would ever apply to him would be "intolerant." When testimony time came, he'd stand up, put about fifteen or twenty love words in the air, and sit down as gently as he had stood up. I always felt his words were like a warm front moving in.

During the week, he worked for minimum wage at a local lumber yard, around smokers and swearers and drinkers. He never rebuked them once as far as I know. He preached no sermons. He didn't have to. His philosophy of life was to witness for Christ, and only as necessary, use words.

Was he intolerant? No. Did he slash and lash out at every signal of sin? No. He didn't need to. His life spoke so loudly that when someone ran into a crisis and needed Grady's Christ, they made a beeline for his side.

He lived out the only kind of intolerance of which we as Christians ought to be accused: the intolerance of a life so dedicated to God that people feel convicted in its presence. It's the intolerance that love has toward hate, that holiness creates against sin. It's the only intolerance that God can condone. When it's properly at work, the unbeliever always feels the love before he feels the rebuke.

4 DON'T BE ASHAMED. DECLARE YOUR TRUE COLORS WITH JOY. (Matt. 7:15-19)

Simone Weil has said that in reality, nothing is so beautiful as the good and true and nothing is so monotonous and boring as evil. In popular culture, these have been reversed. Sin parades around claiming the party. Righteousness is ridiculed as boring and dull. But tell me. Would you swap Hitler's delight for Mother Teresa's? Would you prefer the satisfaction in the heart of a Billy Graham over the happiness in the heart of a Howard Stern?

Granted, much of life is "everlastingly daily" for all of us, believer and non-believer. But if any subset of the population ought to be throwing confetti and celebrating life, it's the Christians. They have found life in the midst of spiritual death, grace in the wilderness. They have overcome the world. They already have a property deeded to them in heaven. They live well. They die well.

Christians face pressures like all people. It rains on their parade. Their children veer off course. Sudden tragedy bolts into their lives and raises a rash of questions. But dig inside their souls, and you'll find a special grace, a grace that helps them absorb the blows and buffer the pain. They can live with conviction because they live by the truth — truth with a capital "T." Robert Louis Stevenson spoke the mindset of the Christian:

> *Away with funeral music set*
> *The pipe to powerful lips.*
> *The cup of life's for him who drinks*
> *And not for him who sips.*

If it weren't for the "ifs" and "buts," the Devil could be a preacher!

Never ever hang your head in shame because you are a Christian. Rather bow your head in prayer because you belong to the King.

5 DON'T BE SLOPPY WITH YOUR CREED; KNOW WHAT YOU BELIEVE. (Matt. 7:7-12)

As boys we used to play marbles. We'd draw a big circle in the sand about the size of a hoola hoop, cock a finger against our thumbs and flick the "shooter" toward the center of the circle. A few boys were known to smudge the line in the sand and ease a little closer to the target.

It is fashionable these days to blur the lines of belief. To some degree, that's needed. We can't be ostriches with our heads in the sand. But neither can we create a giant blob of belief that makes everybody plus God happy. If many moderns could rewrite Exodus, chapter 20, they would have a list called "Any Old Commandments." But God has ten and apparently that's the way He meant it to be.

I have met people whose codes of belief were so scattered that their spiritual lives looked like a venetian blind. The Apostle Paul said, "This one thing I do," not "These several things I dabble at." (Phil. 3:13 KJV)

We are not designed to hold several systems of belief in balance. The very nature of our person craves integration and consistency. When we vote, our inner being yearns to have us vote as one and not to be double-minded. (James 1:8)

A lot of people are struggling with their faith because they are confused by a lot of "add-ons." Like barnacles slowing down a streamlined ship, these "add-ons" are slowing their spiritual progress and keeping them from being their best and most beautiful selves. You may want to alter a line or two in your belief package from time to time, but grab hold of a few principles and lock them in a permanent grip. That stronghold will give you stability when the storms and doubts set in with a fury.

DON'T BECOME FIXATED; BE STATUS GO NOT STATUS QUO. (Matt. 6:19-21)

Ethel Childs was a saint. She lived well into her 90s and watched her church move through at least three revolutions. She was born when legalism was a plague. She was praying when the church faced the iconoclasts of the 1960s who wanted to throw out every tradition older than 1945. She lived long enough to feel the tensions created by the worship and praise chorus revolution. She had plenty of reasons for developing a resistant spirit, but she never did.

During one of my last visits with her in the nursing home, Cousin Ethel, as we called her, summed up her view on faith and change. "So many things have come along that have shaken my world, pastor, that I sometimes wondered if we'd ever make it. It seemed to me as if the church at times was on the brink. But every time I have watched God pour fresh oil into new wine skins and bring new revival to our church. I have personally always sought to keep Christ in control of my life because I figured that He would never go out of date."

A person of conviction is not coerced from without, but compelled from within. He lives from the inside out.

In his book, *A Long Obedience in the Same Direction*, Eugene Peterson says there are two extremely useful biblical designations for people of faith: disciple and pilgrim.

> Disciple (*mathetes*, from which we get the name "Matthew") says we are people who spend our lives apprenticed to our Master, Jesus Christ. We are in a growing-learning relationship, always. A disciple is a learner, but not in the academic setting of a classroom, rather at the work site of a craftsman. We do not acquire information about God, but rather skills in faith.
>
> Pilgrim (*parepidemos*) tells us we are people who spend our lives going someplace, going to God, and whose path for getting there is the Way, Jesus Christ. We realize that "this world is not my home" and set out for the "Father's house." Abraham, who "went out" is our archetype."[1]

There's an old German proverb that says if you rest, you'll rust. Keep moving toward God even if you zigzag at times. It is better to be weaving back and forth going forward than to be squarely on the path but sitting still. Stumble if you must, but keep moving. Swerve if you have to, but keep your heart moving toward home.

7 DON'T BE A CHAMELEON; BE A CHRISTIAN.
(Matt. 7:21-23)

A person of conviction is increasingly bold for Christ no matter what the setting.

A few years ago our family visited the Atlanta City Zoo which has a fabulous menagerie of animal life from all over the planet. We bought our tickets and gathered out front to join the tour guide. We weren't very lucky. The lad who finally showed up to guide us had left his heart at home. From his first words, I knew he was going to dread every step. He resented every question.

His memorized speech was about as exhilarating as a third-grader reciting the Preamble to the Constitution. Rote without thought. When he stopped at the crocodile pit, he punched the button and turned on a tired recording, *"Here is a crocodile."* (Duh!) *"The crocodile is a member of the alligator family. It lives in shallow lakes and lagoons and lays eggs in the sand. When the baby crocs are born, the mother croc digs them out and leaves them to fend for themselves. The crocodile is a long, low, cigar-shaped animal that lives in shallow lakes and lagoons. No, I've already said that."* The recording was skipping.

"Any questions?" He didn't mean it. He moved on. A few steps later he punched the button again. *"Here is a chameleon. It is a member of the lizard family. The chameleon has a tongue as long as its body."* (I had an elementary teacher with that feature.) *"Its eyes can pivot in two directions at once."* (Same teacher.)

"But the most fascinating thing about the chameleon is its ability to change colors to blend in with the background where it's sitting."

"Any questions?" he grumbled, moving to the next exhibit. I stayed behind.

I had heard about these lizards which change colors and I hadn't driven two hundred miles to see that thing sit in a cage looking like it was stuffed. I had noticed that the cage was multicolored, so I decided to test this color change theory. I know you're not supposed to — and I promise I haven't done it since — but I began pounding on the glass like you do on a stubborn Coke machine.

I had to pound quite a bit, but the chameleon finally begrudged me a few steps. It stopped on a section that was green on one end and yellow on the other. Sure enough, within a few seconds it began changing colors to blend in with the background.

Good for chameleons. Bad for Christians.

Show your true colors no matter what the background. In another "Don't Be Attitude" from one of Jesus' greatest followers, Paul draws the bundle together, "Do not be conformed to this world, but be transformed by the renewing of your mind" (Rom. 12:2 NASB).

Every Christian worth his salt has learned to say a few rock-ribbed "no's." Learning to say "no" is part of the process of spiritual growth. Along with the "Be Attitudes," keep the "Don't Be Attitudes" in focus as well. They both show up in the same sermon. Same Preacher. Same faith. They both belong in the same life.

Endnote

[1] Eugene Peterson, *A Long Obedience in the Same Direction*, p. 13.

Mind Movers

1 You sometimes hear it said, "That man or that woman spoke with conviction." What does that mean? Is it a style of speaking or an attitude of the heart? Is that description always a positive one? Explain.

2 Are there people who will probably never be firm in their convictions because they simply "weren't born that way"? Are there people whose very natures make it easier for them to be people with firm convictions?

3 What are specific ways in which a Christian can show himself to be a person of conviction? If a person does not show true Christian convictions when the circumstances demand it, is that person still a Christian? Can a Christian be fickle and still remain firmly in the Kingdom?

4 What is the difference between "being a person of conviction" and "being dogmatic"?

5 How can we be sure to strike a balance between being firm and resolute in our beliefs, and yet loving and compassionate in our relationships?

6 Are teens and children more susceptible to peer pressure than adults? Explain your thinking.

Contribution

Taking Your Turn at the Wheel of Life

Pam Sargeant had never done a ropes course. But the weather was good, the weekend long, the campus dead. Why not? She piled in the van with a half-dozen friends and headed off to the mountain retreat. There within eyeshot of a gurgling mountain stream and a blue dome of sky, she teamed up with three classmates and set out over an intimidating array of obstacles.

For those of you who know the ropes course lingo, these terms will mean something: Wild Woosey, Pirate's Crossing, Tall Ships, Zap Line, Nitro Crossing. For the rest of us, they just mean "scary." And then there's The Wall. Twelve feet of solid concrete. Straight up. No footholds. No grooves. It can only be conquered by teamwork — two members boosting a third, then a hand or leg extended from above.

Pam wasn't sure. She had dragged herself over tires and through a rope net. But over a twelve-foot wall? This was probably the end of the course for her.

> *There's no use going for Christ unless we have first come to Him, and there's no use coming to Christ unless we are willing to go for Him.*

What could they do with her wheelchair after all? Her team members glanced at each other, then down at her. There was a glint of daring in their eyes. No way to go back now. With a deft hoist and a quick shove, they boosted one person onto the wall. They grabbed Pam by the arms and legs and, straining with a mission, they finally hoisted her high enough for her hand to find the reach from above. Sweat rolled from their faces as they folded the wheelchair and passed it up.

For a brief moment, the four of them sat on top of the wall, savoring the heights of victory. Pam lifted her arms and waved in triumph. As they lowered Pam on the other side, the tears and sweat were flowing together. Safely on the other side, they stared back at the wall. It had been their fiercest enemy. Now it stood as their greatest accomplishment.

In this one victory, you can see the four primary supports on which commitment is built.

In order for people to rise to new levels of commitment, they need these four components in place:

Clarity . . . . about the goals and values to which they are being asked to commit themselves.

Pam's plan to scale that wall.

Competence . . . . to complete the assignments to which they're appointed.

In Pam's case, the hands of friends became her hands and joined her heart.

Influence . . . . to make a difference that they can actually see.

The visual memory of scaling that wall will motivate Pam and many others for years to come.

Appreciation . . . . which indicates that somebody noticed and noted their contribution to the cause.

The glance of those friends as they dropped safely on the other side.

The question is never whether people will commit themselves to a cause. The question centers around which causes to commit to and how deeply they will devote themselves. If the Christian faith will show itself for what it is — the greatest cause in the world — it will have devotees who rival Pam Sargeant in their desire. If it will stand up and call people to a life of love and living sacrifice, it will be surprised at now many nominal Christians will become radical Christians.

When you scan the Sermon on the Mount searching for ways in which this Preacher calls on us to contribute, the list covers the full spectrum of life itself. The gifts He calls us to give can't be wrapped and given on one occasion. They are "life-long" gifts, gifts that flow out of our lives day after day.

Jesus offers us at least five avenues of service which naturally arise out of a deeply devoted Christian heart. Let's see how the Preacher calls us to the cause.

1 PRESENT YOUR WORLD WITH THE GIFT OF FORGIVENESS. (Matt. 5:22-26)

In Matthew 5:24, Jesus calls us to leave our gift at the altar and go make things right with our brother. This is an application of the great Old Testament theme, "I will have mercy and not sacrifice" (Hos. 6:6 NIV).

He also says to agree with your adversary while you are on the way (Matt. 5:25), or as one translation puts it, while you still have time. Show yourself to be a real peacemaker just like Jesus meant it here in the Beatitudes. Not just an appeaser of your spirit, but a person who opens yourself up to a deep and thorough cleansing of any spirit of unforgiveness. Jesus was saying to these people, "For thousands of years you have been trying your method of returning evil for evil, but now try mine — returning good for evil. It's just the reverse because my kingdom is the reverse of your kingdom."

A few sentences later in the same sermon, Jesus is back on this theme of forgiveness. He says in Matthew 6:14-15, "For if you forgive men when they sin against you, your heavenly Father will also forgive you. But if you do not forgive men their sins, your Father will not forgive your sins" (NIV). Again in Matthew 5:22, Jesus urges us not to call our brother a fool. The original word for "raca" means "to spit." We are not to spit in the face of another. Take God's offer to help you drop your painful past. Back your past up like a trailer at the landfill of life, unhitch it, and drive away without looking back.

Let me give you an analogy to place in your mental pocket for later use. If you have unforgiveness or bitterness in your spirit toward a person who has hurt you, think of it as a giant block of ice. There it sits inside your spirit, frozen and always lowering your spiritual temperature. As you expose it to the warm rays of God's love through prayer, you melt it a little at a time. Rarely do ice blocks melt all at once. Most often, they melt a layer at a time. As you continue to take that spirit of unforgiveness to God in prayer, He continues to remove it from you a little at a time. Eventually, you will visit the place where that struggling spirit has lived for a long time, and it will be gone. The block of ice will have totally melted and the water evaporated.

If we keep a spirit of unforgiveness hidden in our hearts and refuse to expose it to the warming rays of the Spirit, we lose twice: once when the person perpetrated the sin upon us and again when we allow that person to continue to hurt us by harboring a spirit of unforgiveness. We can refuse to be a victim twice by letting God into this private and painful area of our lives and allowing Him, over time, to help us melt and remove it forever.

Lawrence Sterne, in one of his sermons, wraps this truth in a single sentence. "Only the brave know how to forgive, because a coward could never forgive; it is not in his nature."[1]

A gift of forgiveness lasts a lifetime, not only for the other person, but for our own hearts as well.

2 PRESENT YOUR WORLD WITH VOLUNTARY GIFTS OF KINDNESS. (Matt. 6:1-4)

The little eight-year-old girl squeezed a sermon in a sentence. When the teacher asked, "Students, what is a volunteer?", she replied, "A volunteer is when you lift up your hand!"

Jesus makes this point by exemplifying a phrase that has become synonymous with loving sacrifice — "going the second mile."

In Jesus' time, it was common for a soldier to ask a civilian to carry his luggage. This is illustrated in Matthew 27:32 when a Roman soldier compels Simon of Cyrene to carry the cross. The only trouble was that Simon of Cyrene could not carry the cross the second mile. Only the Savior could carry it from Calvary home.

If we give to others only when they deserve it, we will never give. If we wait to make our contribution until the world beats a path to our door, we will be waiting a long time. The person who makes a contribution to his time must share out of a divine motivation. People will never deserve it. Circumstances may never be right. The only impulse on which to base our giving must be a desire to imitate the generosity of God, Who gave and got badly burned in the process. If we give only by coercion, we will never do it gladly. We will give with joy only when we give for God.

Emily Smith teaches at Berea College in Kentucky. She shares the story of trying to give her dog a spoonful of cod liver oil. Wrapping her arm around the dog's neck, she held on for dear life and guided the foul smelling grease toward his mouth. The dog spun around and jerked free of her hold. Cod liver oil splashed all over the floor. She ran to find a cloth to keep the oil from staining the linoleum and when she returned the dog was licking up the last drop. He liked the oil, but not the method of delivery.

Everything depends on "how" we give. If people sense that we are trying to cram goodness down their throats, they will choke on our gift and resent our Savior. Giving is not only a gift; it is the atmosphere in which we give it.

If you need a quick check test to determine the commitment of Christians, look at their giving. Do they commit themselves and their resources to the cause of Christ? Do they just talk about it, or actually throw themselves into the venture and devote their time and talents to bringing it to pass?

Many people who attend our worship are like people sitting in an airport. They see the television monitors announcing arrivals and departures, they watch the hurry and scurry of people in transit and imagine that they are really part of the action. But more than 25% of people who enter an airport never purchase a ticket or board a plane. If we never fly, we are not risk-takers, but landlubbers. Every person who finally soars for God must snap the surly bonds of earth and touch the face of God for himself.

Today we are big on indoor mountain climbing. Shoot, that's not mountain climbing, that's safety! Real mountains don't have safe inclines and don't guarantee that we'll conquer every peak.

Jesus makes one more point about our gifts of kindness. In Matthew 6:1-4, He tells us to not let our right hand know what our left hand is doing — an idiom of the time which meant, "Don't spend too much time trying to get earthly credit for what you are doing for heaven."

There are four essential motivating factors which lie beneath a Christian's contribution to the Kingdom. At one time or another, all four motivational purposes will come into play in a person's spirit. But one will usually dominate.

aINVOLVEMENT IN SERVICE

The "black hole" in the contemporary church is that we simply fail to act. Indifference is the most characteristic moral dilemma facing us today. Every church has a number of persons who find great satisfaction in the completion of tasks around the church. If these persons are Christians, the satisfaction is especially intense. If these people can be identified and brought to a level of involvement, they are some of the most fiercely loyal and devoted workers the church can have.

Today's congregations are not struggling nearly as much with compromising as they are with *temporizing*, of *hesitating* when they should be *marching briskly forward.*

bASSOCIATION WITH A TEAM

Another group of people find the social bonding with other quality people in the church to be their special source of satisfaction. They are happy to help the church, but they don't really care to work solo. If they can be involved with a group, the personal interaction creates a thriving social energy in which they function and find greatest fulfillment.

Os Guiness speaks of "hollow churches." He is referring to churches in which the unity of the body is lost in a drivenness toward individual stardom.

BELIEF IN THE VISION

This is usually a smaller group of persons who have reflected at a deeper level on the mission and message of the church. They desire to be involved because they sense that their own heart for the work makes a difference. When people function with this type of motivation, they are able to stay on-task in their ministry for the church without extensive outside stimuli.

Such people have forward-looking faith. Their theme is neither "Just as I Am," nor "Just as I'll Stay," but "Just as He Leads."

dLOVE FOR GOD

A very small core of people have arrived at the highest level of motivation — living and serving solely for the glory of God. These people are the prayer warriors, the passion carriers, and the vision givers within the body. God grant that their species will increase.

3 PRESENT YOUR WORLD WITH THE CALMING INFLUENCE OF A CONTENTED SPIRIT. (Matt. 6:32-34)

Jesus must have known that talk shows were coming, especially "hate-talk" talk shows. These are shows with hosts who blather on in the charade of trying to help their guests resolve their problems. Their only real purpose, however, is to titillate the crowd and run up their ratings.

When I channel surf past one of these tabloid talk shows with a host parading as a caring confidant, I always think of that Indian proverb: "Once you've cut off a person's nose, there's no use asking him to smell a rose."

People who listen to these talk shows usually have one of two responses:

- **A RISING SPIRIT OF ANGER AND RESENTMENT.**

     They resent the parade of human abuse guising as entertainment and vow to curb their viewing.

- **A DULLING TONE OF APATHY AND INDIFFERENCE.**

     Another group just shrugs their shoulders and writes such nonsense off as one more inevitable mark of sin on our world.

The withering array of problems that cross our field of vision can leave us equally immobilized. We don't have either the skills or energy to solve them. We go through tunnels of dark futility, wondering how our limited gifts can help us respond to such overwhelming needs.

My car mechanic helped me in this area. I was standing in his shop one day watching him rev the engine (and run up my bill) and discovered something fascinating. He never uses adjustable wrenches. He has enough wrenches on his wall to precisely fit every bolt you can bring him. Whether it's your standard 5/16 or some once-in-a-lifetime 42/145, I'm pretty sure he has it.

But not at my house. I have only four wrenches — all unused and in mint condition. If I need to fix something with a ratio outside my foursome, I have to grab the adjustable wrench. That's the one where you twist that little screw and narrow or widen the grip.

Show poise

Be quiet

Trust God

Most of us have a few areas where we are gifted. Our gifts naturally fit with the task we are called to do. But there are a great many things we are called upon to do for which we have no natural fit. It is a mark of maturity when a person learns that most of life is spent outside of our absolute gift zone. Most things that happen to you will require you to flex, to adjust, to tighten or loosen your spirit before you apply the love.

But flex you can. Don't fret if you don't have the exact gift to do a job or fix a situation. Don't throw your grease towel on the floor if you can't find a fit in your heart. Adjust, flex. Do the best you can and let the grip of the Holy Spirit do the rest.

It is far better to show your world a contented and adjusting spirit than to fret yourself silly trying to find the exact answer. People much prefer a quiet spirit to a petty pickiness.

4 PRESENT YOUR WORLD WITH AN OPEN INVITATION TO CHRIST. (Matt. 5:46, 47)

About thirty years after Jesus' ascension, Paul — his head severed from his body — lay dead at a centurion's feet.

At the moment of Paul's death, the ratio of Christians to non-Christians in the entire world population was 1 to 40,000. Today the ratio of Christians to non-Christians around the world is 1 to 12. That's a striking statistic!

If our generation could influence the world for God like Paul's generation did, the world could be saved in less than eight months! But we are fighting "koinonitis." That's a disease in which the church navel-gazes when it should be out soul-saving. It centers on itself when it should be crying for the world.

"Koinonia" is the Greek word for fellowship, togetherness. It's a good word, but we may have overdone it. "Koinonia" (fellowship) must be balanced with "evangelidzomai" (outreach). We must be always in a spirit of epiphany, SHOWING CHRIST FORTH TO THE WORLD.

5 PRESENT YOUR WORLD WITH A LIFE BUILT ON THE WORD OF GOD. (Matt. 7:24-27)

The Poor Parson asked the right question, "If gold rusts, what will iron do?" Can we agree that there is a remarkable dearth of people who dig into the Word daily? What's gone wrong here? Do we find the Bible dull, routine, boring? Have we lost the ability to stay with anything longer than twenty seconds? The fact is, it takes time to shape your soul in the image of God. This is no snap decision. But what's wrong with a little patience to get something really worthwhile?

I recently heard a young adult say, "I can't be a Christian. Too much discipline and too little fun." Just one fallacy in his comment. He hasn't tried it. Any person who falls head over heels in love with Christ is right in the center of the fun. He loves his study of the Bible. He hates when he can't spend more time soaking up the Word. It's true. Don't let anybody ever tell you differently.

The Carpenter from Nazareth knew about houses and how to build homes that would stand. He knew that flimsy houses could be thrown together in about the same time it took for a storm to blow in. But if the house was going to weather the storms, it had to be more than a lean-to. A house is first built in the heart, then on a blueprint, then into the air. No matter what materials may be laid on the pile, a sturdy house can be built if we build well. It is not the raw materials, but what we do with them that makes all the difference in life.

A Symbol of Hope

In the French Academy of Science in Paris, one display case holds a special story. The awl displayed inside looks ordinary enough, but it isn't. That awl had once fallen from a shoemaker's table and put out the eye of the shoemaker's nine-year-old son. Within weeks, the boy was completely blind in both eyes and had to be enrolled in a school for the blind.

In those days, blind persons read by using large carved wooden blocks which were clumsy and awkward to handle. The shoemaker's son vowed to himself that one day he would create a better system for himself and the millions of others who could not see.

He did. And to do it, Louis Braille used the very same awl that had blinded him in the first place. His system of encoding the alphabet was developed from the awl that now sits like a symbol of hope beneath a glass case in the French Academy.

If we want to make a contribution, we will not always be able to determine what comes our way. But we can determine how we respond to it. We alone can choose how it will affect us. Some people ask, "Why did God let this happen?" Others ask, "How can God help me use this to make a better world?"

Endnote

[1]Burton Stevenson, ed., *The Home Book of Quotations* (New York: Dodd, Mead and Company, 1967), p. 710.

Mind Movers

1 Is there a direct correlation between a person's devotion to Christ and his contribution to the Kingdom? Do devoted Christians make a greater contribution, or does God's grace work through persons regardless of their commitment?

2 Many people who are apathetic about doing anything for God say that they feel their efforts would be futile anyway — that there's so much sin their little contribution wouldn't even show up on the screen. What would you say to a person who feels that way? Is he right?

3 Can unbelievers make eternal contributions to the kingdom of God? Are there unbelievers who do more for God than some believers?

4 What are some of the reasons people fail to make much of a contribution to the Kingdom of God?

5 Will the level of a Christian's contribution to the Christian cause have any effect on his or her future rewards in heaven?

Resistance 4

Have the Courage to Say "No"

Just a few miles north of Boston, Massachusetts lies a bedroom community called Weymouth. It's a gentle, sleepy town with a circle of water they call Whitman's Pond. Each spring the pond swirls with life. Day lilies and brilliant violets wreathe its sloping banks. Birds create a halo of life as they circle above. And then there's the herring — Atlantic herring.

About ten inches long, slim and silvery, they point their faces into the current and head upstream from the ocean. They themselves were spawned in Whitman's pond and nothing short of death will keep them from continuing the cycle of life which began for them in that living pond. Stand on any bridge overlooking that stream into Whitman's Pond and you will see them by the thousands. At times they rest in a side pool; at times their leap falls ten times their length. But always, relentlessly, vigorously, they sacrifice their lives in quest of new life.

In the realm of the spirit, there is no life

Christians are to be Upstreamers in a Downstream world.

without resistance. The person who claims he can indulge any desire and follow any impulse and still remain a Christian has fallen prey to a fatal thought. The truly Christian person says a divine "yes" to Christ, but also says a rock-ribbed "no" to sin.

The sins that swirl around us and beg an invitation to our hearts are relentless. The lure of lust, the tug of greed, the yearning for instant fame, the craving to be more successful and the tendency toward spiritual apathy are forever seeking to bed down in our brains and be lived out in our lives. C. W. Hatch lands squarely on the truth:

> The climate of thought of a given period of history is a most powerful influence and must be reckoned with as certainly as the climate of the weather. Religious conception must be constantly and freshly interpreted in the light of the best knowledge of the time.[1]

I have watched far too many friends forget to flex their muscle of spiritual resistance and end up suffering serious consequences. We are a long way from the days when we were told we couldn't do something "just because I said so." We are a long way from legalism. If anything, the pendulum has swung so far in the other direction that even the church seems to be in moral freefall. When God urges us to resist sin, He is not trying to keep us from something enjoyable. He is trying to spare us from something unenjoyable. Unrestrained freedom brings unceasing pain. Freedom in Christ brings balance and joy.

Applying His Grace at the Point of Our Pain

When we picked her up from a neighbor's farm, she was a fluffy ball of brown fur with two bright eyes blinking at me. I named her Susie. She became the dog that romped her way through my childhood. When I hopped on my bike to go to Grandpa's, Susie was right there on my heels, her bright red tongue lapping up the breeze.

When I grabbed a fishing pole and headed down to the pond, she went along to scare the frogs.

I remember vividly the terrible day when my grandfather was out mowing the hay. Suddenly the field was filled with yelps and howls of enormous pain. Susie had run in front of the scissor-blade mower. One leg was hanging by the skin, the other badly mangled. I stood there at the edge of the field that day, an eight-year old boy looking down into the terror-filled eyes of my best friend. I begged to touch her, but Mom feared she might ravage my hand out of pain. Susie struggled to rise, but had no front legs to stand on. It was the saddest and most graphic picture of helplessness I had ever seen. It is burned on the screen of my mind forever.

Fortunately, a miracle-working veterinarian crafted a new leg and cobbled the mangled one back together. In time Susie healed enough to run and frolic again.

Unfortunately, I've had to see it again and again. I have seen Satan clip the spiritual legs out from under far too many of my friends. I have seen them lying on the ground, battered and shattered, their eyes dripping with the tears of pain. But I have also seen the Divine Doctor at work, applying His healing and forgiveness and hope, daubing His grace at the point of their pain. And people the Devil thought he had mutilated beyond repair, stretched and stood and walked again.

I hope you can feel the compassion of this chapter before you feel the rebuke. Jesus would want it that way. When He urges us to forego something, it is only for our good. If He asks us to say a "no," it is only because He has a better "yes" for us.

In the Sunday school class of my childhood, my teacher would sing a ditty which we thought was downright corny: "Have courage sometimes to say 'no.'" We were real men who could handle anything and here she sat telling us how to say "no." Who in the world did she think she was?

I have lived some since then. If I were a betting man, I would bet that some of those boys who laughed at Mrs. Kay would give their right arm if they could go back and have her sing that ditty one more time. A few of them failed to put a few ironclad "no's" in place and they are paying dearly for the oversight.

Robert Louis Stevenson said that we eventually sit down to the banquet of our consequences. You and I have seen the truth of that proverb. We've watched a teen proceed on the theory that his stomach has the sturdiness of a concrete mixer. So he wolfs down greasy french fries and salty chips and cold baked beans and snubs his nose at a balanced diet. Now here he sits at age forty with his pockets full of Tums and Zwiebach toast in order to soothe a stomach that is now more sensitive than that of a six-week-old baby.

As you listen to Jesus preach the Sermon on the Mount, you hear Him drop direct hints on how to close the door to sin and open it to the Savior. You catch Him urging us to watch out for the wily ways of Satan. You sense His deep desire for us to overcome the world, the flesh and the Devil. Seven times in these three chapters, Christ points out areas where He wants us to say "no" to the current and "yes" to Him. If we line up His advice on the best ways to resist Satan, they look like this.

1 QUIT HURTING PEOPLE, EVEN IN YOUR MIND.
(Matt. 5:21-26)

Jesus is not tiptoeing around here. He is stomping on the hardened clay of our hearts.

Every group of Christians has a favorite set of sins which they deplore with loud lamentation. One group will rant on and on about injustice and discrimination. Another will jump on drinking and smoking. Still others will rail against lying and cheating. But every group of Christians also has a spiritual blind spot. I have seen Christians who were so obese they couldn't get out of a chair without help. Yet they write off a thin smoker as a sinner of the highest order. I have sat in class beside people who made the homeless their religion, but who thought nothing of stealing food from McDonald's in order to feed their friends on the street.

When Jesus bears down on our inner motives, He is watching the same thing. He sees people who wouldn't murder another person with a knife, but who think nothing of skewering them with a forked tongue.

The tongue has killed more people than all the guns and knives and spears put together. If the misuse of the tongue could be curbed, the Christian church would have revival and see the Kingdom spurt upward within weeks. But God cannot bless the mess. He cannot give His full honor to those who have not given Him their tongues. Even infant evil thoughts which we call gossip have no place among the people of God. Gossip begins as a feather and ends up as a full-size goose. Resist the temptation to harm another in your thoughts. Avoid it with as much vigor as you would wish for someone who was tempted to think bad thoughts about you.

No sin works solo. If you harm another in your heart, you injure your own heart. It beats with less beauty. You lower your level of inner peace. For your own sake as well as the sake of others, avoid murder in the mind. It can kill you both.

2 DON'T CRAVE TO POSSESS WHAT ISN'T YOURS.
(Matt. 5:27-30)

It would be hard to find a sin that has more disastrous consequences than lust.

A lustful thought can ruin a lady with a loyal husband and three blond headed kids who are doing well in school. One long glance in the wrong direction can destroy a man with his mortgage paid off and two children in college.

Lustful living leaves a trail of tears and ends at a cliff:

- Lust kills trust.

- Lust ruins family unity.

- Lust leaves children confused and vulnerable.

- Lust causes Christians to backslide.

- Lust makes the victim feel like a failure.

- Lust, once indulged, craves other conquests.

- Lust numbs the person to its stranglehold.

- Lust shatters self-esteem.

Let's not kid ourselves. Jesus is not trying to keep us from having a good time. He is trying to keep us from enduring this list of painful repercussions.

Sin is the only thing in the world that blinds us to its true nature the more we indulge it. If you are caught in a web of deceit, if you have followed the alluring finger of lust, Jesus is calling you. He urges you to spare your soul from hell. He begs you to turn around and close off every association which is destined to damn your soul.

Just because good food is occasionally tossed in the garbage, doesn't mean you have to eat there. I wish there was a gentle way to phrase it, but let's not play around with the very evil that drove Christ to the cross. Craving things and persons which do not belong to us will destroy us, not only in this life, but in the life to come. While you can, run. Run as fast and as far as you can from the traps set by Satan. It is the only way to save your family and to save your soul in the end.

3 CLOSE OFF ANY PLANS FOR DIVORCE AS AN EASY SOLUTION. (Matt. 5:31-32)

Here Christ is calling us to resist a quick out. In our day, many people marry with divorce as an option from the outset. If it doesn't "work out," they will "get out." The Bible doesn't accept that phrasing as marriage in its purest sense. God intended marriage as an unconditional, eternal bonding of lives. Anything less is experimentation with sin.

The fact is, if two people have ever been deeply in love, they can work out most problems. There will certainly be some scenarios which warrant at least separation if not divorce, but this is the rare exception. God meant marriage for keeps. For better or worse. Plus, for every benefit you can think of for why you should divorce, there are probably two reasons why it's unwise.

You can glue two pages of paper together, but when you try to tear them apart, something will rip. When two lives have been bonded by the sacred vows of marriage, they do not suddenly go their separate ways without some damage. Mistrust lingers. Pains work their way deep into the heart. Anger often festers.

In any marriage, the minds of both partners should lean toward staying in the marriage and working things out. Counseling may be necessary, fervent prayer may be needed, sacrifice may be the order of the day. Whatever it takes to resolve our marital difficulties and bring our lives back together under the lordship of Christ, the effort is well worth it. At the very least, let it be said that you gave the marriage a long, strong chance.

If you are in a second or third marriage, you know how much pain can occur when the marriage vows are severed. Of all people, you realize how cautious others should be about bailing out of a marriage until they have given every effort to restoring it with the help of God.

4 RESIST EVERY URGE TO ONLY LOOK OUT FOR #1.
(Matt. 5:43-48)

By its very nature sin focuses you on yourself.

S . . . . *SELF*
I . . . . *INDULGENT*
N . . . . *NATURE*

You don't have to practice being selfish. It comes with birth. Augustine once quipped that if any person doubted the doctrine of original sin, he had not yet lived among humans. We rarely bow to our egos publicly. In public, we set out every other front we can think of. We rarely turn from God in an instant. I have only known two occasions in my entire ministry when persons turned from God to evil overnight.

We give our lives to God with the firm purpose of following Him forever. We start with a heart aimed straight at holiness. But if we neglect our daily disciplines of grace, it is easy for Satan to turn our head — just for an instant.

Paul said that we should live all our lives to the glory of God. But that takes steady effort. We have to intentionally die to ourselves and live to God every day. Otherwise, we can misstep and before we know it, our old habits and old grooves from the past have swallowed us up again.

- If you were critical and argumentative before you came to Christ, you have to stay alert. You will be strongly tempted to return to that spirit.

- If you were haunted by an intense ego before you came to Christ, be careful. That impulse is not dead.

- If you wrestled with lustful thoughts prior to knowing Christ, you can be sure the Devil hasn't rolled over to play dead. In fact, the Devil's very name contains his nature. The Devil is evil. "Evil" is just "Devil" without the "d."

If he can, the Devil will also try to get you bogged down in disputed matters for which there are no sure answers until heaven: arguments about whether Jesus will come back before, during or after the Tribulation; which translation of the Bible makes God the happiest; which guru has the best answers to our tough questions. I still meet plenty of people who want to argue over whether Adam had a navel or whether trees in the Garden of Eden had growth rings. Someone said it well, "Never struggle to climb a ladder when you can see the same wall standing on the ground." Some questions are better left unanswered.

A Subtle, Slippery Path

He may have been sitting on the edge of the crowd, slinking down behind a couple of taller men so the Savior wouldn't see him . . . no, on second thought, I believe he was right down there on the front row.

Let's set the record straight. Judas wasn't born a betrayer. When Jesus picked him to join the Twelve, Judas must have had an attractive soul. He was a young man, genuine, devoted to his family, conscientious in his work, solid through and through. We have to remember that he, along with the other eleven disciples, had "left all" to follow Christ. It may not have been much, just a tattered net and a battered boat, but it was a lot to Judas.

Then Jesus made him the treasurer. Judas carried the purse in which they pooled their pennies. He had a knack for keeping the checkbook balanced. He had never done that before. His father would have sold the fish and divided out the few drachmas to provide for the family. He had always paid for the cloth and food that Judas needed. But not now. Now Judas was holding real money in his hands. He can hear those coins clinking together as the purse bounces at his side. He dumps the contents out into his upturned palm, making sure they have enough for another meal.

Then one day he takes just one tiny coin for himself. Just one. He would pay the purse back on his next visit to his parents. Then another penny. A fishcake here, a palm fan there. Nothing big. But every little sin weakens his resolve and glazes his eyes.

Finally his big chance comes. The Sanhedrin will pay him thirty pieces of silver if he will lead them to Jesus. What a wonderful opportunity. He will get the money in advance. Jesus will escape. Pure profit. Plus the Sanhedrin deserves to lose their dirty money. They need this lesson.

It's the subtle slippery path of putting our own plans and wishes above those of principle. It is living by the line, "I can do it better than God."

Judas needed to hear the adage, "Where a drop can go, a river can follow."

5 REFUSE TO YIELD TO THE TEMPTATION TO BE EARTH-SMART BUT HEAVEN-DUMB. (Matt. 6:19-24)

Here in Matthew 6:19-24, Christ turns our eyes upward. He merges the divine world and our daily world. These two worlds interface. The person who lives only for this world is really living to die. The person who lives with eternal values in view is living to live.

There are too many people who think more about their homes than they do about their hearts. They will spend hours making sure their homes are immaculate and leave their hearts smothered in dust.

The extreme emphasis on the physical body in our culture is sad because it is not balanced with an equally avid devotion to the spiritual self. To many, eternal life has become having the perfect body in this world. They give no thought to what will happen at the hour and article of death, when their physical bodies will return to dust, but their spirits will return to God.

This is no reason to indulge the body as if the way we treat it makes no difference. For the Christian, the way we take care of our bodies reflects our overall commitment to the stewardship of God's gift of life. But those who focus on the body to the exclusion of the spirit have set their sights too low.

I am not making excuses for being dirty and slouchy. I remember my embarrassment at taking friends to visit one Christian lady's home. It looked like the local dump. Calling her house a mess was like calling a bomb a firecracker!

The call is for balance between this world and the next. And the decided need in our time is for more awareness of the next — to lay up for ourselves treasures which will outlast a beautiful bicep or a gilded mantle. In the classic, *Tenders of the Flock*, Leo Trese writes:

> It is a strife and a struggle to keep ourselves unworldly, unsecular. By the very fact that we do live in the world, we are continually exposed to the steady pressure of its thrust. A vague and general intention to have no part in worldliness is not enough. Day by day, by repeated acts, we must beat back its well-concealed compulsion.[2]

6 RESIST THE THOUGHT THAT AN OPEN DOOR IS THE RIGHT DOOR. (Matt. 7:13-14)

It is the Devil's way to make the door so broad that you can't help but see it. If we are easily guided, it is easy to assume that the open door is God's invitation. But the example in Matthew 7:13-14 makes just the opposite point. In biblical times, just as today, not everybody lived in tiny houses and huts. Wealthy people could afford porches and verandas and large columns decorating the front of their homes.

Jesus had probably seen several homes in Jerusalem which paraded their wealth with ostentation: ornate columns out front for all to see, massive doors swinging from elaborately carved posts. The peasant people were duly impressed and must have stopped often on their journey to admire the beauty and splendor of these mansions.

But Jesus urged caution. He knew that behind those splendid doors often lay a home full of chaos and pride. He knew that the servants who slipped in through the private back doors were often much happier than the people they worked for. They were "saints in Caesar's household" and they were laying up treasures in heaven where neither moth nor rust would corrupt.

In these gripping verses, Jesus paints the larger picture to make the point. "Enter in at the straight gate, the back gate," says He, "which leads to eternal life, and not by the glamorous glitzy front door which looks appealing, but once inside, that's all there is."

In order to know God's will, we must exercise God's gift of discernment. To assume that a certain relationship is God's will just because it seems to be flowing along smoothly is dangerous. To assume that we should walk through a door of opportunity because God has not dropped an iron bar across our path is equally risky. We must use discernment. Whether the opportunity seems appealing or repulsive is not the issue. The issue is the wider will of God which must be discerned after prayer and counsel with Christian friends.

There's an imp in impulse. The natural tendency would be to take the wide open opportunity and then seek to make it fit the will of God. But the narrow way may well be God's way. Never mistake the door for the interior. The Devil's door looks appealing, but just inside his compound is a lake of fire.

7 RESIST THE QUICK FOUNDATION. BUILD YOUR LIFE A DAY AT A TIME ON THE WORD OF GOD.
(Matt. 7:24-27)

The foolish man in this parable finished his house first. He didn't waste time building the foundation and footing. It has never stormed here, he was told. There's no danger.

Into every life there come storms. The person who has not prepared for them lives to regret it. When the dreaded moment leaps upon him, he cries out for mercy, but often the plea comes too late. All the care in the world cannot save us if we have chosen a personally shallow and superficial life.

We may have laughed at the elements. But they can be merciless. We may have bragged that we could weather the storm in our own strength. But only those who have been through the storms know how frail human strength is against the severity of the elements. The only way to ensure the best passage through the fierce storm is to build a secure foundation which is not vulnerable to the storm.

Never join a cause with no laws.

In this sermon, Christ is telling us to resist the Devil in order that he may flee from us. He knows that resistance alone will not make us holy. But He is also teaching us that repentance means at the very least that we turn away from sin. There are laws of safety which we obey to our benefit.

Purity comes both from saying "no" to sin and "yes" to the Savior.

Have you seen the "ocean" lately? Not the blue one. The gray one, the vast churning ocean of cultural values. It heaves, lurches and foams with talk-show froth. Western culture has left the shoreline and is bobbing like a cork on a windswept sea, in a pagan-black night. It is darker than any Dark Ages you ever heard about in history class.

Go back a thousand years to another shining sea of moral chaos. The whole Mediterranean world which our teachers tried to etch into our minds was convulsed with abortions and apathy, church crooks and feuds, "holy" wars and horrors. Knights wore shining armor over treacherous hearts. They gathered for crusades but more were doomed than saved. It was a millennium of madness.

But if you strain your eyes across the darkness of the centuries, you'll spot a few things that refused to drift. There upon that hillside, with a valley amplifying their sound, Gregorian monks are tuning up their hymns of praise to God. On that skyline is a spire pointing to its Maker and honoring its builder. Around it, the air is foul and dark. It is the Dark Ages.

Listen with both ears cupped and you can hear Augustine, a few decades earlier, talking about two cities, one of them the dust-doomed city of the plain, the other the permanent Paradise of God. A bit more tilt and you will hear him saying that the citizens of the world are restless until they find rest in God. Centuries later, as the Crusades come to a close, Geoffrey Chaucer is praising a pilgrim who chose to voyage against the odds.

There's plenty of "culture" to wash you away. But where sin abounded, grace did much more abound. When evil surges toward the shore, grace still tides it away. If there are days when the whole world seems awash in the tumbling tides of sin, keep an alert eye. Look to the spires and to the city of God with its thousands of beachheads in the world. And be sure to look down and celebrate the solid rock beneath you. It may be dark, but if the light of God is shining down on you, there's always plenty of light to see around your feet. You can be sure of your steps. You need never flounder in a vast ocean without knowing exactly where to find the rocks that will guide you to another shore.

If you are developing proper spiritual resistance to the world, the flesh and the Devil, these things will be true of your growing commitment:

> ## A Growing Commitment means that . . .
>
> . . . *you have chosen one way over the many ways*
>
> . . . *you care less and less about more and more*
>
> . . . *the Devil's investments in you are meeting with diminishing returns*
>
> . . . *the salvation of your soul is being followed by the salvation of your mind*
>
> . . . *feelings are built on faith and not the other way around*
>
> . . . *your witness for Christ has steadied from a flicker to a flame*
>
> . . . *Sunday is a rehearsal for Heaven, not a reminder of hell*
>
> . . . *you are gaining altitude in a freefall world*

Endnotes

[1]C. W. Hatch, *Stewardship Enriches Life* (New York: Abingdon, 1968), p. 30.
[2]Leo Trese, *Tenders of the Flock* (New York: Sheed and Ward, 1955), p. 42.

Mind Movers

1 The capacity to say "no" to sin can be strong or weak. What weakens a Christian's ability to resist the Devil?

2 Can a person be in a continual pattern of sin and still be saved? Does being saved mean that a person does not commit deliberate sin?

3 The Bible urges us to "Resist the Devil" so that he will run away from us. What does that mean?

4 Our resistance to sin is stronger at some times than at others. What preventions should we take to turn away from evil in the times when we feel especially vulnerable?

5 Is it easier for some people to say "no" to sin than other people? Explain.

6 What "values" in our culture today need to be strongly resisted by Christians?

Serenity 5

A Calm in the Eye of the Storm

You may have heard about the visitor from Germany who stepped into a phone booth late one night to call and get his bearings. He looked high and low and couldn't find the light. A passerby realized his dilemma and stepped over to help him.

"Here, let me help you. You need to close the door." The passerby grabbed the folding door, pulled it closed and the light blinked on.

No telling how much confusion we could spare ourselves if we would enter into the closet and shut the door. Entering the closet is one thing. Shutting ourselves in with God is quite another. If we're honest, we would probably admit that we sometimes make it to our prayer place, but we still don't see the light. The door of our mind stays open to the long "To Do" list — the unresolved problems, the noise of silence.

Serenity is like a butterfly. If you flail your arms and pump your legs in a nonstop chase for it, you probably won't catch it. If you want it, you need to sit quietly and in time it will glide over and rest on your soul.

People search for peace in a great number of places where it can't be found. It can't be found in:

1 MORE MOTION

Did you hear about the pharmacist who was criticized for staying on the job and not getting out to see the world?

"Don't you ever get tired," somebody asked him, "of slaving away at this job all day? Don't you ever hate it that you can't be out enjoying the party?"

"No," he replied, "but I sell a lot of medicine to people who do!"

No wonder the Preacher by the sea urged his audience not to worry (Matt. 6:25). If you have to move ten inches to be happy, you won't be happy when you arrive. If more motion made for more happiness, we would be a culture of ecstasy. The typical person today travels by air, land and sea an average of 24,500 miles a year. In 1950, the average was 6,500. You can get motion sickness just keeping pace with your day planner.

That's why the Bible is forever calling us away from double-mindedness — having a mind with all kinds of conflicting loyalties. Every once in a while Jesus pioneered a way off the beaten path. Probably nowhere is that pioneering clearer than in His call to a single-focused mind.

A person who is double-minded has at least two reasons for everything he does. He has a good reason (which he announces) and a real reason (which he keeps to himself). Single-mindedness is not narrow-mindedness or simple-mindedness, but a kind of genuineness, a soundness at the core, an indifference to externals.

Wendell Price says, "There are many activities I must cut out simply because I desire to excel in my pursuit of God."

In his *Utne Reader* article, "Why An Empty Hour Scares Us," Stephan Rechschaffen is picking up a clear signal. "The pressures of modern life are such that many people become anxious and uncomfortable when they find themselves doing nothing. Instead of perpetually rushing, people should take time out to let their rhythms slow down."[1]

Unrealists assume that you can always be in the right place at the right time and always on top of things — always on top of the pile. But whoever said that being on top of the pile was the plan of God? That is not life. Life is full of piles. You may be on top of a few, in the middle of a few, and some of them you may need to shovel! But the point is, you can live with piles.

There's really not much room for motion in a closet with a shut door. Did Jesus choose the smaller room because he wanted us to quit wiggling around for a while?

Serenity is also not found in:

2 MORE THINGS

In 1950, families claimed in a survey that they needed 14 household gadgets and wanted another ten. In 1995, that number had shot up to 37 "needed" and another 16 "wanted."

I find it intriguing that the description of heaven in the book of Revelation portrays a simple life: a clear sparkling stream flowing out from under the throne, a tree loaded with fruit, a sky flooded with the light of Christ, streets paved with the purest and prettiest of metals. And every feature of heaven responds to the great needs of life — water to drink, food to eat, a sky to contemplate and a solid foundation on which to walk.

As Jesus unfolded his Sermon on the Mount, He called us to a simpler life. Don't worry about food. Don't worry about clothes. Don't worry about things. Then He drives the point home. "Your heavenly Father knows that you need all these things" (Matt. 6:32).

If you have quite a bit of month left over at the end of your money, maybe you are more into things than you think. Next time you are rummaging in the attic for a suitcase, look at the number of things stashed there that you never use. If you hadn't been looking for something else, you would never have even known they were there.

Last year I wrote to Chuck Swindoll and asked him to prepare a five-minute video to share with students and ministers at a conference here at the university. His return letter was as warm and as personable as I had come to expect in reading his books. He declined the invitation with these words:

> *Dear Joe,*
>
> *Thank you for the invitation to speak to your conference by video. I am honored to be asked.*
>
> *My wife and I sat down last year and decided to rearrange our lifestyle. I've been trying to churn out books at the rate of three a year, speaking at too many places and trying to juggle in a round or two of grandparenting. I am busier than a one-armed paper hanger with a case of poison ivy.*
>
> *When we sat down to decide our strategy, we only had three criteria: simplify, simplify, simplify. We even boiled those three down to one: simplify. You probably understand that all too well. Thank you for understanding my need to decline.*
>
> *I pray your conference will be anointed by God.*
>
> *With sincere joy,*
>
> *Chuck Swindoll*
> *Dallas, Texas*

In the fall 1995 issue of *Psychology Today*, the results of a twenty-two-year longitudinal study show that there has been a substantial decline in ego integrity over the past two decades. The study concluded that while materialism was emphasized in the 1970s, today there is more emphasis on meaning. Low marks are given to politicians, big business and religion in terms of credibility and trust. Wise marketers are highlighting trust and credibility as never before.

Can you simplify your life and give more room for the spiritual? To integrity? To simplicity? To the quiet, inner world of the soul? Do you need to spend less time adding to your collection and more time in your mental carpet slippers?

Peace and inner joy will never be found in:

3 MORE NETWORKS

If we don't have peace on the inside, a list of friends as thick as the phone book won't make it happen. In our "Kleenex Kulture," many people fall into thinking that if one relationship doesn't work, they can chuck it and get another one. Blow their nose on it, so to speak, and throw it away.

Nothing Doing!

I stopped dead in my tracks. We were on our way into the ceremony, groomsmen and bridesmaids all in a row. In an unguarded moment the groom snickered to his best man, "Well, I figure if this woman doesn't work out, I can always get another one."

I whirled and stared him straight in the eyes. "John, unless you confess that comment right here on the spot, I refuse to open that door and enter the sanctuary. I will have nothing to do with a temporary commitment."

He may not have changed down deep, but he prayed as good a prayer as a man desperate to get married could pray. All through the wedding he kept giving me that nervous look that said, "You're pretty serious about this thing, aren't you?"

There's a big difference between relationships for profit and relationships for enrichment. One exploits; the other ennobles. One discards; the other redeems. In a world where it's easy to step on people on our way up a human staircase, we need a whole new generation to see the Kingdom in its inverted form and take the words of the Preacher seriously, "The greatest among you will be your servant. For whoever exalts himself will be humbled, and whoever humbles himself will be exalted" (Matt. 23:11, 12 NIV).

Peace and contentment will never show up in:

MORE DATA

Our society is trying to do something horrible to us. It is trying to turn us into gatherers of data rather than keepers of relationships. I have dear friends in the ministry who would rather spend the afternoon in cyberspace than care for their flocks, and God help them. We must turn off the TV and love the people around us. We need to click on "Exit" and enter the real world. We need to scan the paper and read our family.

They call ours the "information age." Like the ice age before it, the information age will run its course. Old Testament ceremonies were taken seriously in their time, but eventually they ran their course. God phased out the ceremonies and phased in His Son. He returned His people to the heart of all growth and development — relationships. The ceremonies had become rote, so the Word became flesh.

In the Sermon on the Mount, Jesus tells us what to avoid. He also tells us what to embrace. Every sermon balances "do's" with "don'ts." The King of Preachers does it well.

There is another "MORE" list which aligns itself with the heart of God and the Sermon on the Mount. To find more serenity, we need:

MORE VIRTUE

Here are six sure characteristics of a virtuous heart:

- A virtuous heart is forever seeking out things which endure.
- A virtuous heart is forever searching out things that enrich the mind.
- A virtuous heart is forever scouting for truths to engage the mind.
- A virtuous heart is forever investing in eternity to endow its future.
- A virtuous heart is forever pursuing new ventures and embracing new friends.
- A virtuous heart is forever enforcing its chosen virtues.

In virtuous living, there is always something deeper on the inside than anybody ever sees on the outside. A person of virtue has decided to give God what Eugene Peterson, author of *The Message,* calls "a long obedience in the same direction."

BMORE BASICS

If the Sermon on the Mount is anything, it is basic — core cut right out of the heart of the gospel. No piddling at the edges here. It is right down the center line of Christian living. From start to finish here are the basics that Jesus addresses:

The Blessed Life 5:1-12
Our Influence 5:13-16
The Value Of The Bible 5:17-20
Our Relationship With Others 5:21-26
Fidelity In Marrriage 5:27-32
Telling The Truth 5:33-37
Love And Justice 5:38-48

Giving To Those In Need 6:1-4
Prayer And The Lord's Prayer 6:5-15
Fasting 6:16-18
Preparing For Heaven 6:19-24
Worry And Contentment 6:25-34

Judging Others 7:1-6
Praying Persistently 7:7-12
The Gate To Heaven 7:13-14
The Fruit Of A Holy Life 7:15-23
Wise And Foolish Builders 7:24-28

If I could have only ten chapters from the entire Bible and had to lose the other 1,179, I guarantee you I would include at least Matthew, chapters five through seven. They contain every theme central to the teachings of Christ. They are the ABCs, and they will help you be an ABC person: **A**lways **B**e **C**hristian.

If you need a ready reference at any point along the way, start with this sermon and you'll likely find out what Jesus would do in a particular situation. It is that fundamental to the rest of His teachings. In fact, this

Sermon takes about 20 minutes to read. The entire corpus of Jesus' teachings (what is printed in red in many editions of the Bible) can be read in two hours. You can see what a high percentage of Jesus' actual words appear in this one message.

In a Discovery Channel special, Wayne Gretzky, arguably the best hockey player of all time, recalled the Saturday morning when his dad taught him a lesson in hockey away from the ice. The Gretzky family had gathered for a family reunion at Grandma's house, a white clapboard house that sat on a sprawling farm.

It was five o'clock on a Saturday morning when the sixteen-year-old Gretzky heard a knock at the door. "Son," his father called, "wake up and come out here a moment. I want to show you something."

Wayne said he could not imagine what in the world his father wanted to show him at five o'clock in the morning, especially on a Saturday morning. Nine o'clock was more normal. Wayne pulled on a pair of pants and walked to the old screen door on the front porch. His father was standing there with a face full of purpose.

"Son, I want you to see this." Wayne looked to where his dad was pointing. There at the side of the old farm house knelt his grandmother in her flower garden amidst seedling marigolds, hyacinths, crocuses, and petunias. With caring and careful hands she was stirring the soil and spreading the brown wrap of life around the roots of her infant flowers.

"Son," Wayne's father said, "You are a talented hockey player. I wanted you to see this picture for future reference. Your grandmother is kneeling here at five o'clock on a Saturday morning to make sure that she has a pretty flower bed that perhaps 25 people will ever see. Son, you will probably play before millions of fans. If your grandmother can work this hard to bring beauty to 25 people, surely you can be equally dedicated for 25 million."

"There are times," Wayne observed, "when I am skating late in a game, my legs aching, my mind weary with trying to outsmart the opponents, and that picture of my grandmother comes to mind and I take new energy from that memory and the words of my father, 'Surely you can be equally dedicated for 25 million.'"

No matter how far God takes you in life, never forget the basics — that handful of eternal truths around which you have built your life of faith. They will never be outdated, outmoded or outdone. Keep them always before your face in an uncluttered view.

The peace of Christ gives us:

MORE PERSONHOOD

You cannot program the Holy Spirit nor budget the grace of God, but you can make yourself available to Him so that more of His Person flows into your person.

We live in a time when it is easier to be "humans doing" before we are "human beings." In our culture of productivity, it is too easy to define a person's worth by the thickness of his wallet. In this shallow culture, the people who are most at risk of being eliminated from life are those who can't add to the bank roll — babies not yet born and older folks liquidating their assets.

But God never said to Adam and Eve, "Unless you make four more fig leaf skirts by this time tomorrow afternoon, I'll have to fire you and get another couple to start My world." His only request was that they come and walk with Him in the garden in the cool of the day. Their worth did not rest in producing fig leaf skirts, but in taking walks with God.

One day when my close friend David and I were boys, we were playing near Holiday's barn at the edge of the pasture. We discovered a calf that had slipped outside the fence, just outside of its mother's reach. The mother was mooing in a plaintive way, wanting her calf to come back, but the calf could hardly stand, let alone make its way back through the fence. David and I carefully nestled the calf in our arms and walked along the edge of the fence toward the gate, the mother cow following us at an anxious gait the whole way. When we finally released the calf back into her care, the cow licked and loved on that little tike as if she had missed his company for years.

A whole pasture full of grass could not make a cow contented when she was separated from her calf. And a whole screen full of data cannot satisfy the deep need for another person who truly loves and cares. Our great need is relationship. Our greatest relationship is with God.

Another key to personal peace is:

MORE GOD

Please don't miss my point. Finding God does not require the solitude of a prayer closet or the isolation of a monastery. This is not an appeal for hermits. Closets may be needed for balance in our spiritual lives, but God is not locked in a prayer closet. It was not mortuary quiet where Jesus lived. He was the Christ of the maddening crowd. His prayer in John, chapter 17, was not that His people be cocooned from the crowds, but that they be kept in the crowds.

There is much literature that tells us to find God in the country or in the meadow or in a sylvan paradise. But the Bible never calls us there. Even when Jesus tried to catch a few private moments at a well in Samaria, He wound up ministering to others.

The place to find God in your schedule is in the busiest fifteen minutes of your day — when five people are asking for ten things all at once. If God can't work there, then your God's too small.

Francis Schaeffer, in his book *No Little People*, drowns out the background noise with his clear call:

> Quietness and peace before God are more important than any influence a position may seem to give, for we must stay in step with God to have the power of the Holy Spirit. If by taking a bigger place our quietness with God is lost, then to that extent our fellowship with Him is broken and we are living in the flesh, and the final result will not be as great, no matter how important the larger place may look in the eyes of other men or in our own eyes.[2]

Jesus found His Father in the very parts of His day when the crowd's noise was the loudest:

- *A woman had to bump His disciples out of the way in order to reach through and touch the edge of his cloak.*
  (Luke 8:43-48)

- *He performed His first miracle at a raucous wedding reception.*
  (John 2:1-11)

- *A handful of men had to break through the rooftop to get the paralyzed man within reach.*
  (Mark 2:1-12)

- *Jesus healed a man who couldn't get through the crowd to find a place in the Bethesda Pool.*
  (John 5:1-15)

- *Jesus made the blind man see not seascapes and landscapes but milling, arguing, pushy people in the alleyway.*
  (John 9:1-12)

- *Our redemption was accomplished in a crowd — a jeering, shifting crowd, scheming and thirsting for a bloody mess.*
  (Luke 23:1-39)

Jesus found God in settings as crowded as a department store the day after Christmas. He was the Christ of the crowded way. If your days are incredibly busy, that is about the right pace for God. If He could create the world in six days, He is used to being busy. That's His natural element too.

The more we have of God, the more we love each other. It is a fundamental rule of thumb that grumpy people are shallow people. The fuller we are of God, the less room we have for criticism and grouchiness. The more we mature as Christians the less we insist on specific answers to every question. We don't demand that a body of Christ believe exactly as we do, or else we will pout and threaten to leave unless they change.

Look carefully into the text for the spirit of these words from R. E. Ewin:

> Loyalty to the group is not simply a matter of expecting it to come up with the right answer more often than not, which is pretty much the case in my relationship with my doctor, but more often feeling that they care about the right things and make their judgments, even when they are mistaken, in terms of those values.[3]

When we say that God is a person, we are doing more than mouthing a proper theology. We are reminding ourselves that through faith we are in touch with a person. Faith is a person nearby. In touch. At hand. It doesn't take long to figure out that maintaining a strong spiritual life is a lot like bowling: accuracy improves with closeness. The closer to God, the closer to life. True life. Abundant life.

Under a Father's Watchful Eye

Les McClelland pastors in New York. He tells of a memorable day back on the farm of his childhood. His father had let him drive the tractor for the first time. Les had watched his dad steer that old Farmall up and down the rolling hillsides for years, but today he would get to drive the tractor by himself. His father ran through a few final instructions, cranked the engine and stepped off and over to the edge of the field. Les said he felt powerful, trusted, secure. As he slowly let the clutch out and the tractor surged forward across the field, he could feel the pride rush up his throat. He glanced back to be sure his dad was watching.

And then the knoll. It was just a slight rise in the field, but as Les crested the knoll and started down the other side, he looked back and his father had disappeared. He was hidden by the hill. Les panicked. What would he do without his father's watchful eye? Could he turn the tractor around?

He did finally turn the tractor around at the end of the field and headed back toward the barn. Les relates, "I stood up as I drew near the hill so I could see my father sooner. As I came up over the hill, there he stood, the most wonderful dad I had ever seen. I had driven the tractor out of sight and back again and there stood dad smiling his pride and approval."

If there are times in your life when you feel you have crested the hill and left God behind, never fear. He knows the way that you take and if need be, He will hurry over the hill and help you. Maybe, just maybe, He trusts you so much, He's giving you a chance to show Him that you can take the right turns in life without having to have Him there nudging you every second.

Endnotes

[1]Stephan Rechschaffen, "Why An Empty Hour Scares Us," *The Utne Reader* (January-February 1994): 64.

[2]Francis Schaeffer, *No Little People* (Downers Grove: InterVarsity, 1974), pp. 22, 23.

[3]R. E. Ewin, "Loyalty and Virtues," *Philosophical Quarterly* 42 (October 1992):412.

Mind Movers

1 Is all the talk about ours being a "rat-race, hectic" time just so much talk and not really true? Do you think too much is made of people being super busy today?

2 How do you explain that certain unbelievers seem to be more contented than others who say they belong to Christ?

3 Why are people who exude joy and peace of spirit so appealing to us?

4 Is a person who is racing to make ends meet and keeping up with all the needs of a family eligible for true serenity? Or do we need to be honest and acknowledge that he will probably need to wait for peace until he is nearer retirement?

5 What steps can a frantic and restless person take to attain a greater spirit of inner serenity?

6 Is it possible for a person to remain peaceful in his or her spirit all the time? How can a person learn to lean on God and not fret so much about the details of life?

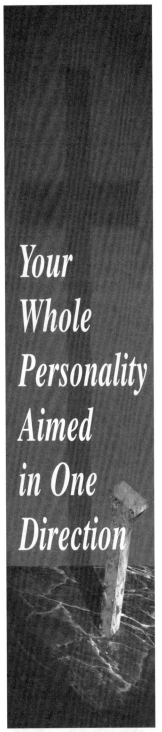

Convergence

Your Whole Personality Aimed in One Direction

By today's standards, the Sermon on the Mount is brief. But the Preacher that day wasted no words. Standing there in the middle of the congregation on a hillside by the Sea of Galilee, Jesus composed a masterpiece. In less than half an hour He covered every dimension of the human spirit — behavior, belief and being. At the end of the message the people were amazed, not only because they got out of church on time, but even more "because he taught as one who had authority, and not as their teachers of the law" (Matt. 7:29 NIV).

If you gather a group around you today and read them this sermon, 95% of the time they will nod their approval to the words. Remind them of their role as salt and light and they will agree. Challenge them to love their enemies and they will say "Amen." Tell them to give to the needy and — while they may grunt and groan on their way to their wallets — they will give and live to brag about it.

No heart is pure until it's passionately pure. No virtue is safe until it's radically safe.

But there are two verses in this sermon where you will lose some, two verses that clash with the shallow spirituality of this present darkness. If you read these two verses aloud, even to Christian people, they will elicit reservation. "Nice idea," they will say, "but not too realistic today. Maybe back in the days of Conestoga wagons and large front porches and flour being ground at the mill, but not today."

One of these "hard" verses sits squarely in the middle of the Beatitudes, and the other comes at the end of Christ's reflections on the nature of divine love. These verses are twins:

Matthew 5:8: "Blessed are the pure in heart, for they will see God."
Matthew 5:48: "Be perfect, therefore, as your heavenly Father is perfect."

That's a pretty tall order. If you are a thinking person, these verses give you pause. But we have to start with the conclusion that if Jesus hadn't meant them, He wouldn't have put them in. When you only preach twenty minutes, you don't need filler. These verses aren't in here as catchy little lines to wake up a drowsy crowd. They are here because they capture the greatest single need of the human spirit — a clear, pure focus; a laser-sharp love.

We may argue over exactly how it looks in life, but we can't argue that God wants us to be perfect. The person who is clear in his focus, pure in his vision, sees God. Who wouldn't want that? Who in his right mind wouldn't want to be pure in heart and squarely focused on the lordship of Christ in his life? What Christian wouldn't want to keep God in "perfect" view?

Friedrich Nietzsche didn't see many things

The gift of sprawl is never trophied. What is trophied is focus, passion and zeal.

correctly. But this one thing is an exception. In writing about devotion to a cause he noted, "The essential thing 'in heaven and earth' is that there should be a long obedience in the same direction."[1] That mood of long obedience is the very mood which the world, with all its swirl, is forever trying to annul.

Today a good number of people in the Christian movement are living out what we might call "compartmental Christianity." Holy here and careless there. It's an unwritten policy of Christian living that contains these elements:

> - Become a Christian, but don't go overboard.
> - Live just above the average of other Christians around you.
> - Realize that you can never be perfect in this life.
> - Keep your Christian walk practical; avoid being too spiritual.
> - Be realistic. We live in a different world than Jesus did.

Dropping a Bomb

On a flight out of Charlotte, North Carolina, I plopped down in seat 21A right beside a man in his middle sixties who was born to talk. He set up in-store delis for Wal-Mart. Before he could even fasten his seatbelt, he was in full stride. "Had a fine woman in the hotel with me over the weekend. This is a fine place for women. I hope they send me back here again."

I didn't say a word. On and on he rambled. Eat, drink and be merry. Go for the gusto. About five minutes into his parade of females, his job and his upcoming retirement, he finally took a breath. "You look like a fine upstanding young man. What do you do for a living?"

I had been hoping he'd ask. I turned right toward him so I could catch that first look when I dropped the bomb. "I'm a minister."

He never batted an eye. "That's great. I'm a Sunday school teacher myself. Last Sunday we talked about the three Hebrew boys in the fiery furnace. Great story."

I was stunned. The bomb had dropped all right. In my face. Call girls and Hebrew boys all in the same breath. I couldn't reconcile them. Sunday school rooms didn't belong with night clubs in the same sentence, let alone in someone's life.

"But, sir," I said, looking right at him. "I thought you said you were with another woman. Are you married?"

"Oh, yes, fine woman. Thirty-seven years. Don't know what I'd do without her. I don't tell her about my little fun on the side. Wouldn't want to hurt her feelings."

I mentioned the ethics of it all. "Well, pastor," he was as cavalier as ever, "you know we can't always do what the good book says. You gotta' have a little fun sometimes."

He rambled on for several more minutes trying to argue himself into happiness. By the time he was finished, I had figured out that all the talk was his way of covering up a lot of guilt and a growing regret that his wild oats were ripening for harvest. On first impression, he sounded happy, jovial, contented. But I listened long enough to hear James' words ringing in my other ear: "He is a double-minded man, unstable in all his ways" (James 1:8 NKJV). I shuddered to think how I would feel if that man taught my Sunday school class next Sunday. When a person can divorce his behavior from his belief and sense no shame, he can teach all the Sunday school classes he wants, but the Kingdom of God is diminished!

When Christ calls us to purity of heart and perfection of motive, He is not warbling in the rafters. He is zeroing in on the need for inner personal focus, the need for a unified inner life. It is the single greatest spiritual transformation that we will need in order to be at home in heaven. He is saying that the happiest people are fully integrated people, not just focused in any old direction, but focused solely and fully on God. They are people who have a fixed obedience in the direction of righteousness.

The Sermon on the Mount points to three specific dimensions of our personality which need to be brought into alignment around the righteousness of God — three features of our lives which need to be submitted to the lordship of Christ. While all three of these components of personality are interlinked, they are also sufficiently distinct for us to deal with them one at a time without losing a sense of their unity. In the points of his sermon, Jesus highlights at one time or another all three:

1. Behavior	**"What we do"**
2. Belief	**"What we think"**
3. Being	**"Who we are"**

God wants us to be molded into His image in all three areas — behavior, belief, and being.

1BEHAVIOR

The most visible part of our personality is our behavior. How we conduct ourselves creates our public self. Our actions, reactions, feelings, lifestyle — all of these are what others see. But living with ourselves as we do, we know that our behavior is only the tip of our personality. So subtle is God's handiwork in our personality that we can honestly fool people into thinking we are good all the way through by the way we behave on the outside. You've heard these words a hundred times, "How could he have done such a thing? He was such a nice person. I never would have believed it."

An article in *Reader's Digest*, "Kidnapped by a Rapist," described Richard Starrett of Martinez, Georgia, as "a decent man devoted to his wife, Michelle, and year-old daughter, Mariah." Then the skin-chilling phrase, "But Starrett lived a double life." The rest of the article will ripple your spine. It tells of a string of murders with glee, abuse and misuse of every young lady who fell into his deadly trap. To a neighbor, the question ran like a record through her mind, "How could he have done such a thing? He was such a fine father and husband."[2]

Threadbare

Jesus had seen it dozens of times — a devout Pharisee standing in the Temple with his prayer shawl draped loosely around his neck. At each end of the shawl were 613 strings, each one representing the specific rules which the Pharisees had developed to cultivate their legalism. The man would stand conspicuously in the Temple, draw each thread up to his lips with the prayer, "I will obey." Each time his lips touched the string, the line was the same, "I will obey."

But Jesus saw it differently. "These people honor me with their lips, but their hearts are far from me" (Matt.15:8 NIV).

Nothing is more beautiful to behold than a fully consecrated life expressing itself in a string of holy deeds. When behavior flows out of the deep holy intentions of our hearts, the radiating waves of kindness spread out to create a halo of influence which only heaven will reveal.

BELIEFS

But behavior alone doesn't tell the whole story. Just beneath the surface of our actions lies our motives, our beliefs. This package of beliefs contains our assumptions about life, about God, about our purpose in the world. It also contains a thousand other less important matters such as the colors we like, our attitude toward government, preferences in food and clothing. Our beliefs, big and small, form a layer of life just underneath our behaviors. Unless we decide otherwise, our behaviors usually rise straight out of our beliefs. That is God's natural plan. Only by intentional deception do we separate our behaviors from our beliefs.

When we invite Christ into our lives, when we make room in our beliefs for belief in Him, that single new belief is so powerful that it begins to influence every other decision we make. Bad habits start to fall away. Healthy habits step in to take their place. Bad attitudes of resentment or bitterness or hate bump into this new divine energy and create a sense of inner discomfort. We sense that they need to go. That's why we call conversion the beginning of a radical experience. The longer we live with this new belief in Christ pulsing in our lives, the more we realize that He is out to claim every part of us. The fact is, there is no sanctification except entire sanctification. What kind of holiness would not be entire?

Christ will not co-rule. Either you're in or you're not. But not to worry. God will not strong-arm us just to throw His weight around. It is God's way of restoring us, bit by bit, to the original perfection which He initiated in the Garden of Eden. He offers us His power to help us take the steps that eventually bring our complete personality into conformity with His will. Squeezed into a sentence, salvation is nothing more nor less than God's divine process of getting us, in the end, back to the beginning — the way He intended when He started the human family.

That's where this third dimension of personality restoration comes into play. As Jesus unfolds the points of His message, He keeps returning to the matter of our being: who we are, way down deep, beneath our beliefs and behaviors, right at the core of our person.

BEING

Between the bookends of our behavior and our beliefs is our being. It is the largest and most influential component of the three.

Jesus moves beyond dealing with sins to dealing with sin, beyond attitudes to the very leaning of our will. He knows the innate tendency we have to veer away from God, the elemental compulsion that shapes our beliefs and behaviors in the first place.

If there is one great need in the evangelical community, it has to be this: for Christians, who have allowed God to begin reshaping their behaviors and beliefs, to invite Him to go one step further and begin a major renovation of their deepest being.

Today's Spirit-filled youth have come up with their own set of delightful terms to describe what God is doing for them:

- **I've Got My Camera Focused.**

  Not just turned in the general direction of God, but both aimed and focused. Holiness is more than a nod to God, it is a fixed posture of the soul.

- **I'm Living In The Upper Deck.**

  Straight out of baseball card mania, this term indicates a life that refuses to live on a low level of spirituality when the upper deck — nearer to the realm of God — is accessible.

- **I'm Swimming In The Deeper End Of The Pool.**

  One student went on to add, "In the shallow end of the pool you can stand on your own feet, but out in the deep end you have to depend on God."

The fall of Adam and Eve in the Garden of Eden so affected the personality of the human family that we are born with a severe inner leaning away from the will of God. "There is no one righteous, not even one" (Rom. 3:10 NIV).

In the greatest sermon ever preached, Jesus drives right to the point. I want your behavior to be holy, I want your beliefs to be holy, and even more, I want your very being to be holy. We will not finally have a righteous mind, we will not finally live a righteous life unless we ask God to give us a righteous will. Our will is aimed in the wrong direction. It must be reversed by the divine head of God as an act of His grace.

In Luther's simple analogy, a man can shave his face as close as he wishes, but he will have to do it again tomorrow. Only by having a complete removal of facial hair will the problem of shaving go away.

Many Christians are frustrated because they yearn to live a more consistent

Christian life but they are forever stumbling back into old mindsets and pesky habits. This makes them wonder if they ever knew God in the first place. Of course they did. Fretting about their salvation is worrying in the wrong direction. The issue before them is not that of having Christ save their souls; the need now is for Christ to reorient their wills — that part of the self that got turned around by the original sin of our parents and has been aimed away from God ever since.

In order to find true inner spiritual focus, the being needs to be transformed by God so that it is brought into full alignment with our behaviors and our beliefs. All three need to be aimed in the same righteous direction. People may struggle with whether or not God can work that deeply in their lives. But those who have asked God to help them in all three dimensions have found profound alignment of life and a joy in their inner worlds. It makes you wonder why anyone in their right mind would refuse God entry to the deepest levels of his life.

Can you think of any good reason why a person would let God enter his life as Savior but hedge on Him going any further? Why let him in the front door and then refuse him access to the rest of the home? You can talk about Christian growth. You can talk about Christian maturity. If you will invite God to work with your inner will to bring it into conformity with His original plan, the immediate improvement in your behavior and beliefs will be striking. You will sense the difference right away.

You've probably ridden escalators, those moving stairs that make another floor as simple as a step away. When I was seven, I fell in love with escalators at a giant Sears store in Greenville, South Carolina. I never got over it. I still love to ride these moving stairways. I'm a little old to play on them alone, so now I take my children with me. While Mommy shops, we play "Up and Down."

But pay attention to this. There are two ways to take the escalator from the first to the second floor. You can either jump on the escalator coming down and run like crazy to overcome the downward flow of the steps which are forever pulling you back. Or you can take two steps over to the stairs that are going up, run at the same speed, and be on the second floor in less than half the time.

When we first come to Christ for salvation, we are hindered by the fact that while we have begun our upward venture with God, we have a strong inner pull in the opposite direction. Our very inner being is pulling us back. It has been so detoured by original sin that it has a strong gyroscopic tendency to steer even eager Christians back into the grooves of sin. One man explained it another way: "I feel like a chameleon standing on plaid!"

Once the initial euphoria of salvation subsides, many people flounder in a time of confusion. They feel they made the right decision, but they find it is easier to begin than to continue. They struggle for consistency, struggle with wildly sinful and scary thoughts which flash across their minds, feel the frightening tug of old habits winking and beckoning them back. It can be a time of intense inner doubt.

It's at this juncture, when the awareness of the inner downward pull becomes painfully obvious, that the Christian needs to open up his life for a genuine change of being. It is at this very point where he needs to turn to God, not just to forgive his sins, but to reorient his being.

It is a time for letting God turn man's sin-bent will into a God-bent will, for reaching down beneath his behaviors and beliefs to fix the problem at the very core — his being. Once God works at the "being" level, we begin to experience a true inner alignment. To use our escalator analogy, our desire to move upward and onward in God is enhanced by a new inner surge of our own God-aligned will to move us in the same direction. Our minds are not fighting our wills, but moving in tandem with them. Now our behaviors can more naturally bring honor to God, because we have been made "perfect" and "pure in heart."

Because of the proximity of our culture, we will still be tempted to sin. An escalator has sections which, if you hold on to them, can pull you back in spite of the steps which are ascending beneath you. It's an imperfect world and at times you will get snagged on the escalator. But you will be surprised at how much easier it is to live for God — and with greater consistency — if you will go for the "Change of Being" which God can bring about in your life.

Even when the remaining human struggles and occasional wobbles cause you frustration, the "Change of Being" brings a deep inner desire to become more and more like Christ. You find a surging divine power to help that happen. The double-mindedness which James refers to is overcome by a compelling new desire to go in one direction. The sins and habits which once tripped you up so easily (the "besetting sins" which the author of Hebrews mentions) now have far less power to hinder and dominate your life.

Commitment means living your life one God-honoring decision at a time.

God wants to guide our behaviors. God wants to shape our beliefs. But most of all, God wants to transform our being. He wants to bring the full range of our personality into harmony with His divine plan for personal joy and spiritual happiness.

Is that a stage of spiritual change that you want in your life? Do you know any reason why you shouldn't let God deal with you at the core of your being? What would keep you from beginning a prayer for this kind of deep and pervasive change today?

Endnotes

[1]Eugene Peterson, *A Long Obedience in the Same Direction*, p. 13.
[2]Peter Michelmore, "Kidnapped by a Rapist," *Reader's Digest* (December 1994):108.

Mind Movers

1 Life is not as simple as it used to be. Our great-grandparents traveled at the same speed as Abraham and Paul. Messages were communicated by methods centuries old. Look at the following list and evaluate the general impact of these modern inventions on the Christian faith:

> TV
>
> Radio
>
> PCs
>
> Internet
>
> Wall Street
>
> Books
>
> Public Schools
>
> Satellites

2 One man said, "I live in three or four different worlds and find it hard to bring them all together." What did he likely mean by that statement?

3 With all the ethical choices that we face today, is it possible to see every decision as black or white? Are there ethical areas which are so fuzzy that even mature Christians have difficulty knowing what to do? Explain your answer.

4 What does Jesus mean when He asks us to be "pure in heart"?

5 Does someone who lives in a home with unbelievers have it more difficult spiritually than a person who lives in a home in which every person is a Christian?

6 Can a deep devotion to Christ help a person overcome depression and pessimism or are Christianity and psychological struggles unrelated?

7 Can you truly say that all of your life is under the lordship of Christ? If not, what would prevent you from giving all of yourself to Him?

Stability

Standing Firm in an Avalanche World

I was in a hurry. It was already 7:40 in the morning, and class started at 7:50. Ten minutes to drop off my two children, Mary Joy and Joseph, at school, race to the office and scoot on to class. I planted two kisses and ran back to the van, jerked it into reverse and — thud! — I slammed into a solid steel post. It stuck up just high enough to catch my bumper but not high enough to catch my attention.

I panicked, thinking I had hit a child. I dashed back to see. Relief. Relief that I had only struck a pole and doubled my bumper up under the fender. Then a second wave of relief. Less than two feet behind that steel pole sat a gorgeous stained-glass window. I sure wasn't happy about my bumper, but that steel pole and its echo on my bumper were beginning to look like an act of my guardian angel. I made it to class on time and had a first-rate devotional — about stable steel poles and bent bumpers and protected windows.

Let's admit both facts. Nobody likes a bent bumper. But I'll sure take a dented bumper to a broken window, a hand-crafted stained-glass window given by a major donor! If I had to pay to fix either one, I'd pay for the bumper any day!

Whether it's the truth of God in the Bible or the truth firmly embedded in our hearts, we are extremely fortunate to have such a fixed pole around which to focus our lives. We may sometimes bump into it and have our egos bent, but how much better to be corrected now than doomed later.

E-G-O. It means

E . . . *Edging*

G . . . *God*

O . . . *Out.*

Commitment to Christ brings with it an openness to His rebuke and correction in our lives. We ask for His guidance in our lives, fully aware that it may mean sudden jolts if we move out of moral line. When we lurch forward under our own power, we may be stunned by the spiritual slap on the hand. "For whom the Lord loves He corrects" (Prov. 3:12 NKJV). As we mature in the Christian faith and fight off the pseudo-gospel of total tolerance, we see our correction for what it is — a stabilizing thrust by our heavenly Father to keep us from careening out of spiritual control. If you meet occasional correction, you are fortunate. It means that God, forever the Gentleman, is honoring your request to hold you steady in a world where morality is in freefall all around us. A commitment to Christ is an invitation for Him to bring His divine power to keep you upright and stable in a teetering world.

A number of insights can be tethered to this stake of spiritual stability.

1 Stability Means That Some Things Are Non-Negotiable.

Look at this list of fixed truths which our culture thinks it can move and be none the worse for the dare.

- ## The Uniqueness of the Christian Faith

   A recent article in an Ivy League journal which promotes one world religion was entitled, "When God Speaks in His Other Voices." The article argued that the great faiths of the world are leading us up several sides of the hill, but all are leading to God.

- ## The Deity of Christ

   The latest twist is that Jesus is not only not divine, He has been made out to be a fabrication. He is a composite put together from the lonely brains of a group of disciples, who never did have a leader, but just made one up! He is a creature they morphed out of their minds to console their souls.

- ## The Value of the Church

   "Church" is just a mindset, so they say. Not an actual gathering of people. Why gather with a bunch of people you don't even like? If you believe in the priesthood of believers, why not access God directly and bypass the boredom. It's a subtle lure.

- ## The Need for Prayer

   With Christians praying on average about two and a half minutes a day, they don't have a large enough sample to draw any conclusions about the value of prayer.

Grab a rubber band and stretch it between your index fingers. If your left index finger represents the eternal truths of God and your right index finger represents the direction of your soul to or from God, which way are you moving right now? Are you drifting farther away from God and putting tension on your connection with God? Or are you moving toward God and finding greater and greater joy in moving more and more toward His peace-giving mindset? The closer you move to Him, the less stress of the "rubber band" of life.

You may move toward God or you may move away from God, but you will never move God. The joy in your Christian life will depend entirely on the direction in which you are moving.

2 Stability Implies That You Will Encounter "Moral Migrants."

Moral migrants are people who will like your views for a day, but sneer at you for planning to stand by them for a lifetime. They are people who pride themselves for having held every view under the sun, but who shudder if you insist there's only one way — and a narrow one at that — to the Father.

Ravi Zacharias writes about a radio talk show he hosted in Ohio. One caller was already angry before she got on the line. "All you people have is an agenda you're trying to promote," she began. She dove straight into her pool of frustration, "With this abortion issue, all you want to do is take away our rights and invade our private lives."

> ## You may move toward God or you may move away from God, but you will never move God.

"Just a minute," Ravi interrupted her, "I haven't even mentioned abortion."

"So where do you stand on abortion," she fired back.

"Can I ask you one question?" he replied. "On every university campus I visit, somebody stands up and says that God is evil for allowing evil in this world. The person says something like this, 'A plane crashes; thirty people die and twenty live. What kind of God would arbitrarily choose some to live and some to die?'"

He went on, "But when we play God and determine whether a child within a mother's womb should live or die, we argue that as a moral right. So when human beings are given the privilege of playing God, it's a moral right. But if God plays God, it's immoral. Can you explain this to me?"

She blathered on for a few more seconds before she hung up.[1]

If our commitment to Christ is to count for eternity, it can't be as brief as an encounter with the offering plate on Sunday morning.

Culture says	sit down and don't rock the boat.
Christ says	***stand up for the truth and if the boat tips over show the people how to swim.***
Culture says	go with the crowd and have a ministry of friendship.
Christ says	***be enough of a friend to tell the truth.***
Culture says	go with the flow and save your energy.
Christ says	***be an upstreamer in a downstream world.***

Even a passing glance around our culture opens our eyes to a number of stray philosophies which are converting our society to a mindset of "moral migrancy." Beginning around 1900, modernism spread its wings and began soaring over the religious landscape. With its flight, a widespread sense of the miraculous disappeared. Eclipsed by its dreadful shadow, Christianity seemed to become just a religion-in-general, just one more option on the menu of world faiths.

In the middle 1900s, a new brand of religious thinking — and we must be sure to call it religious and not biblical — began to grab hold. Called neo-orthodoxy, it elevated the person and lordship of Christ, but lowered the credibility of the Bible. It claimed that the Bible was a fallible witness to the revelation of God in Christ. That subtle but serious divorce of Christ from His Word set off ripples of cynicism which are still widening across the world today.

Beginning with the cynical 1960s, humanism became the opiate of the people. All of life was reduced to a series of processes — natural processes without the need for God. In the late Carl Sagan's famous line to Larry on Larry King Live, "The universe as we know it began with a very pregnant atom."

Today we are awash with naturalism which praises nature and diminishes the uniqueness of the human being in the global plan. Far from being the manager of the garden as God intended, humankind is now seen as just another link in the food chain, and a rather dumb — if not a missing — link at that.

Jesus saw it coming. "Watch out," he warns in this sermon, "for false prophets. They come to you in sheep's clothing, but inwardly they are ferocious wolves. By their fruit you will recognize them" (Matt. 7:15-16a NIV).

3 Stability Urges Us To Make A Decision Before We Actually Confront One.

Not every time is a good time to make a decision. Not every setting is an ideal setting in which to make a choice.

When the passions are high . . .
> When the attraction is intense . . .
>> When the temptation is in full gear . . .
>>> When the Devil is dressed to kill . . .

. . . is not the time to make a decision.

There are two clear phases to any moral situation. In the first phase we make the right decision from a fairly objective and Christian point of view.

PHASE ONE: WE MAKE A DECISION.

But there is a second phase when the energy of the enemy begins to gather around our minds and we realize that we are rapidly moving toward a moral crisis. If we linger too long before we decide in which direction we will go during temptation, the Devil's odds of winning our wills are high.

PHASE TWO: THE DECISION MAKES US.

I wish I had a dollar for every time I've heard the words, "We just got carried away" or "I just couldn't help myself."

It takes a moment to save the soul, but a lifetime to save the mind. Just so you don't miss it, it takes a moment to save the soul, but a lifetime to save the mind. Have you found that to be the case?

When working with young people I always say,

> **FORM**
>   **FRIENDS**
>   **CAREFULLY**
>   **BECAUSE**
>   **FRIENDS**
>   **FORM**
> **YOU!**

During the summer, our family usually takes in a theme park or two. We like the ones with those double and triple hump slides. You grab a gunny sack, line up behind the masses and wait. The line finally dwindles down to you. Sack in hand, you are still in control. Even after you toss it on the metal slide, you can still back out. You might bruise your ego, but at least you can back out. But not on the third hump! When you're airborne and screaming out your last will and testament, you are in no condition to plan your landing. You lost control about two bumps back. Your best hope now is to pray that you land with most of your limbs within easy reach. Smart people look before they leap. They ask about consequences. They judge the risks. And they do that *before* they reach the point of no return.

In moral matters, accuracy improves with distance. (Not in bowling. In bowling, you want to get as close to the pins as you can.) But in moral decisions, the closer we get to the actual dilemma, the less likely we are to make the right choice. Decide well in advance how you will respond in a particular moral moment. You will be the winner for God if you will have a "Decision Crisis" before you face the "Moral Crisis." If you make the right choice at the "Decision Crisis," you will have one less crisis to manage.

It needs to be noted for balance that at any given time in our spiritual lives, we are on a continuum of spiritual maturity. There are, in fact, phases of commitment. We must always be sensitive to those who may not yet be as mature as we are in the truth. On the other hand, we should not despair if we find ourselves behind many others who seem to have a firmer grip on good and on God.

One of the best models for showing the several stages of Christian commitment is the account of the woman at the well, found in John, chapter four. Take a moment to read this passage of Jesus' witness to this lady and then see if you don't sense, even in her short meeting with him, how she moved quite rapidly through these several stages of commitment. Most people today do not experience such rapid commitment; that is simply the nature of our culture. But her model of surrender to Christ mirrors how we also find ourselves drawn more and more to His might and majesty.

See if you can spot these stages in her coming to Christ.

THE STAGES OF CHRISTIAN COMMITMENT:

Stage One . . . . **Hesitation**

Stage Two . . . . **Openness**

Stage Three . . . . **Appreciation**

Stage Four . . . . **Acceptance**

Stage Five . . . . **Admiration**

Stage Six . . . . **Adoration**

Make your decision for Jesus first, then your decision to choose His will second. The rest of your choices will track you closer and closer to the person you want to be. Remember, it takes a moment to save your soul, but a lifetime to save your mind. Keep saving it one God-honoring decision at a time.

4 STABILITY RESULTS FROM HOLDING VALUES THAT ORIGINATE IN THE MIND OF GOD.

A meandering spirit has taken up residence in many of our churches today. Many people in our day are like the pilot who sets his gauges incorrectly before he leaves the ground. The higher he climbs the more inaccurate they become. The problem is not where the gauges are, but where they started from. No wonder Jesus said in Matthew 6:19, "Do not store up for yourselves treasures on earth, where moths and rust destroy, and thieves break in and steal," and Paul echoes in Colossians 3:2, "Set your mind on things above, not on earthly things."

> The lure of a consumer culture is the . . .
> . . . temptation to be *Relevant*
> . . . temptation to be *Spectacular*
> . . . temptation to be *Powerful*
> . . . the *"Now-Wow-Pow"* syndrome.

Everybody is committed to something. Environmentalists in Sedona, Arizona are so committed to the natural environment that they persuaded the McDonald's there to color its arches teal!

Deep commitment creates a stabilizing balance in life. God has so designed us that we need a deep commitment to someone or something. It is His plan for that Someone to be Himself.

True biblical stability has many imitators. But sincerity of heart is no substitute for commitment to the truth. You can step in front of a Mac truck sincerely hoping that you will be safe, but you have still stepped in front of a Mac truck.

As I mentioned earlier, we have no shortage of spirituality in our time. Being "Jesus people" was popular in the 70s. Being "born again" was popular in the 80s. Being "spiritual" is popular in the 90s. Faith is flying all over the place. Fans "believe in" Garth Brooks. Patients "have faith" in their doctor. New Agers parade their merger with the universe. (I saw one I'm pretty sure had made it — or else his butter had slid off the biscuit!)

90

Faith is plentiful. Christian faith, however, is in shorter supply. We have faith on the same principle that champagne knocks the cork out of a bottle. We can't help it. What we can help is the object of that faith. A vague, nebulous faith, scattered and splattered in a dozen directions may be popular, but it's worthless in the long haul. No, worse than worthless. It's damning. False faith displaces true faith and leaves nothing permanent on which to build an eternity with God.

> Let us stand firm on our convictions:
> - *We believe in the Incarnation, but not reincarnation.*
> - *We believe in free will, but not as you will.*
> - *We believe in diversity, but not in a diversity of deities.*

To be in good standing at the end of things, we have to begin with the truth which had its origin in the mind of God. Be sure not to settle for stability based on the wrong object. It is possible to climb a ladder which is leaning against the wrong wall. Bank your faith in the character of God alone.

5 STABILITY IS POSSIBLE BECAUSE OF THE DEPENDABILITY OF GOD.

If God were fickle,
    faith would be a moving target.
Since God is dependable,
    faith is an anchor for the soul.

If God altered His standards,
    faith would be a guess in the dark.
Since God is consistent,
    faith is a reach with a grip.

If God were unpredictable,
    He would be no better than the rash of wannabe gods.
Since He is completely reliable,
    He stands alone as the final point of reference for faith and life.

In our school days, we became familiar with what teachers called our "Permanent Record." Somewhere deep within those great gray filing cabinets, they had the scoop on us. If you made an "F," it was there, flashing like a strobe light for all the world to see. If you made an "A" in art, it was also there, adorning your name. But it was a permanent record. Short of an act of God (which was often prayed for but rarely received) that record will exist for a long time after you have left school.

Be careful! We live in a time when many assume they have no Permanent Record and that they can indulge in any behavior they want and start all over tomorrow. It is a nonchalant attitude spawned by the reign of relativism. If God operated like that, we would jump on His case. We insist that He be the same yesterday, today and forever while we flit like fireflies — as if yesterday and today had no connection and how we lived yesterday makes no difference today.

An Unlikely Building Block

We usually call him the saint with the short fuse. He sat at Jesus' feet the day He preached the Sermon on the Mount. Jesus had His eye on him. In time He would give Peter the keys to the Kingdom and put this veteran fisherman on the front lines to catch men.

Peter was from a wide spot in the road up in Galilee. That won't mean much to you until I show you what Josephus said about the Galileans:

> They were fond of innovations, and by nature disposed to change. They delighted in treason and betrayal. They were always eager to find some new leader and help with an insurrection.[2]

Does that sound like the man you want running the company? Does that sound like just the person to put in command of the committee? A true blue friend for life? Hardly! And yet it was just this man — whose very nature and culture argued against him being the main leader — that Jesus placed smack dab in the middle of the pack of His disciples. Along with James and John, he was one of the rocks on which Christ would build his church.

I remember what one critic said of H. G. Wells' novels: "They begin strong, go on gathering fury for a good third of the book and then sit down like a soggy brown baked apple." That nearly describes Peter's loyalty. But Jesus saw something better in him, believed in him, kept His grip on him when Peter had lost faith in himself. In time, this waffler became a rock, as firm and as dependable as the Christ on Whom he had built his life. When the winds blew and the rain beat upon his house, it stood firm — for Peter had built upon the Rock.

6 STABILITY MAKES FOR CONSISTENT LIVING WHEN THE PRESSURE IS ON.

> *A tree is grown from the roots,*
> *but*
> *A tree is known by its fruit.*

Compromise makes a good umbrella but a poor roof. It is a Band-Aid which is often useful in politics but is never the sign of integrity.

In our pursuit of righteousness we must not be unrighteous. Being on our way home is no justification for tramping through a flower bed. That was Jesus' gripe with the Pharisees. They weren't consistent. They talked out of both sides of their mouths. They claimed to love God out of side one, but hated their brothers out of side two. So He called them by a term whose meaning is hard to miss — hypocrite.

A hypocrite is an actor. The Pharisees of that time often made their faces unsightly on purpose. They put ashes on their head so that men might know they were fasting and admire them. A few probably did. But Jesus blasted the play-acting. Christianity was the real thing. It didn't need any actors. In a scathing rebuke, Jesus denounced the Scribes and Pharisees for their hypocrisy. In His famous "Seven Woes" passage, Jesus called them blind guides, whitewashed tombs, snakes, and a brood of vipers (Matt. 23:1-33 NIV).

Many people will miss heaven by about 18 inches. They know Jesus with their lips, but they never met Him in their hearts.

7 STABILITY MEANS THAT YOU SEEK OUT AND STAND BY THE THINGS THAT ENDURE.

The Russian philosopher Nicholai Berdyaev, said that the foundations of

Western Society are shifting. Things long held sacred by use and need are shifting. Nowhere is there enough solid earth underfoot. We are living on volcanic ground with eruptions possible in any realm at any time.

In the Sermon on the Mount, Jesus speaks of a broad way that leads to destruction and a narrow way that leads to eternal life. This image comes from the mansions of that time which had both a large front portal or porch through which many people could enter, and a narrow entrance through which only a few guests could come. When the time for the festive family banquet came, the large front porch was closed off and the invited guests came in through the "narrow gate."

If we wish to enter heaven, we will have to possess the faith which endures and the name which insures our entrance there — the name of Jesus.

John Wesley sounded the horn of hope: "Give me one hundred men who hate nothing but sin, and desire nothing but God and I will shake the world."

Or look as Robert Louis Stevenson moves a step beyond a child's garden of verses:

> To a man who is of the same mind that was in Christ, who stands at some centre not too far from His, and looks at the world and conduct from some not dissimilar, or at least not opposing attitude, every such saying should come with a thrill of joy and corroboration; he should feel each one below his feet as another sure foundation in the flux of time and chance; each should be another proof that in the torrent of the years and generation, where doctrines and great armaments and empires are swept away and swallowed, he stands immovable, holding by the eternal stars.[3]

Is stability a mark of your spiritual life? Are you standing firm in an avalanche world? Are you at risk from the raging waves of sin that surge around us?

Has the rock moved?

A Lesson from a Suitcase

Cal Emerson lives in Michigan. A few years ago he was a salesman for Adidas. He was successful, comfortable. His business had him living out of suitcases, but the money made it worthwhile. His children would have the best.

One day on his whirlwind pass-by home, Cal did what he had

done a hundred times before. He threw his open suitcase on the bed and left it. His son Brad, age six, knew what that meant: Dad was packing for another trip. Cal could see the disappointment in his eyes. As Cal was headed down the hall, he bumped into Brad and spoke without thinking, "Brad, do you want to go with Daddy on the trip?" The little boy lit up like a lightbulb. "Yes, yes, yes!"

"Well, go and get in my suitcase," Cal teased, not meaning it. Brad dashed to the bedroom.

Half an hour passed. Cal had totally forgotten their conversation. As he stepped into the bedroom, he stopped short. There in the open suitcase sat Brad, eyes sparkling, gearing up for the trip.

That did it. Standing in the doorway, Cal crossed a greater threshold than money, power, and upward mobility. Nothing could compete with the pull on his heart of a little boy willing to sit in a suitcase for half an hour to be "with Daddy."

Cal resigned at Adidas, opened the door to ministry and put his family first. God has honored his decision with a far better paycheck than you can earn on paper — a family devoted to Christ.

"At the time," he said later, "it was a tough decision, but the longer I live, the more sure I am that that day in the doorway of my bedroom was a day when God helped me close a door on earth so I could lead my family through the door of heaven."

Endnotes

[1] Ravi Zacharias, "Just Thinking," Fall 1995.
[2] Josephus, *The Wars* (New York: Harper & Row, 1817), p. 422.
[3] J. A. Findlay, *St. Matthew* (New York: Richard R. Smither, Inc., 1930), p. 35.

Mind Movers

1 Do you believe that, on average, a Christian person is more balanced in his personality and lifestyle than an unbeliever?

2 If a Christian does not feel very confident in his life, should he hide his struggle to some degree so as to make the Christian faith appear to really work?

3 Should a Christian read the Bible and pray daily, or is that just a helpful habit taught by a few leaders but not really needed for deep spirituality?

4 Think of one or two of the more stable Christians you know. What do you believe contributed to their consistency and stability?

5 What are a half dozen benefits of a mature and stable Christian faith?

*Fitting All
the Pieces
Together*

Holiness

8

One of the most challenging questions on holiness today has to do with how and when this experience comes to us. Many claim it's progressive. Others are sure it's mainly the grace of an instant. Most agree that it has elements of both. So who is right?

If you travel south on I-26 out of Asheville, North Carolina, about 20 miles south of Asheville, a large green sign on the right side of the road announces:

> Eastern
> Continental Divide
> 2130 Feet

There are stretches along the Continental Divide where the Appalachian Mountains rise to a sharp peak. If you stand at that point on a rainy day, you can tell within seconds of a raindrop hitting the ground which way that drop of water will go. If it falls to the east, it will flow out to Cape Hatteras. If it falls just to the west of that defining line, it will flow to the west and eventually blend with the mighty Mississippi on its way to the Gulf of Mexico.

There are other stretches along that mountain chain, however, which are nearly level plateaus on top. The mountains have no sharp peaks. They level out and run for miles in several directions in an almost perfect plain. If you stand near that section of the Continental Divide, you will have to wait much longer to see which way a single drop of rain will flow. It might zig one way for a day, then turn and trickle back in the opposite direction before finally finding a stream cascading down the mountain. But no matter how long it takes, that drop will eventually course down the mountain.

The person who comes to God often has faith that God can bring him to a point of inner holiness in a moment of time. And he is not disappointed. Others take longer to come to a point of fully consecrating their lives to God. But they all eventually arrive at the same point. If we let the details of an experience keep us from the beauty of an experience with God, we have stopped short of His best. The Devil would be pleased to have us get bogged down in the minutia of the steps to holiness.

Just because there are dozens of styles of worship doesn't mean that any one of them is invalid and worthless. Just because there are several suggested methods for how to be fully given to God does not mean that we should throw out a whole biblical doctrine. The people who discard holiness over the issue of progressive vs. instantaneous are looking for an excuse, not a holy life.

Watch as the Preacher opens His heart on the subject of holiness.

1 A HOLY LIFE WILL MAKE YOU POPULAR WITH THE CROWD THAT COUNTS.

"Blessed are you when people insult you, persecute you and falsely say all kinds of evil against you because of me. Rejoice and be glad, because great is your reward in heaven, for in the same way they persecuted the prophets who were before you" (Matt. 5:11-12 NIV).

Most peer pressure is pressure about how we appear, what somebody will think of us in terms of this world's values. We all want and need acceptance from others. But that desire must come second. Our first priority must be to aim toward God because "great is your reward in heaven" (v. 12).

We too quickly settle for pitiful praise. We pause for human applause.

We make the mistake of assuming that the loud praise of men is more important than the quiet praise of God. We try to maintain a residence in both the world of the flesh and the world of the spirit. The two aren't on the same planet, let alone in the same community.

Luciano Pavarotti, peerless tenor of the opera world, shared this story in a television interview. As a young man, he trained for several years with a professional tenor in his hometown of Modena, Italy. At the same time he attended a teacher's college. Pavarotti came to a crossroads for making his life-long commitment. He asked his father, "Shall I be a teacher or a singer?" His father replied, "Luciano, if you try to sit in two chairs you will fall between them. For life, you must choose one chair."

Jesus Himself said, "No one can serve two masters" (Matt. 6:24).

Perhaps we are not yet convincing because we are not yet convinced. Hebrews 11 is about a faith that counts. And costs. Has yours cost you anything lately?

A HOLY LIFE WILL MAKE YOU A SOURCE, NOT JUST A REFLECTOR, OF RIGHTEOUSNESS.

"You are the light of the world. A city on a hill cannot be hidden. Neither do people light a lamp and put it under a bowl. Instead they put it on its stand, and it gives light to everyone in the house" (Matt. 5:14-15).

God is not just a God of transactions. He is a God of transformation. He changes us from the inside out. Jesus slips inside our hearts to make His point. He drills right into the center of our spirits and pours in His own holy Self. It is this truth more than any other which ought to cause us to dread the thought of sinning and crave the thought of righteous living.

Do you remember those young years when you snuck around behind your parents' backs? They said "no." You spent time trying to figure out how you could do something sneaky without getting caught and without hurting them — just for the fun of getting away with something. The instant they showed up, you stood tall, faked a smile and pretended that you had just come from the counsel of angels. Their actual presence made an instant change in both your behavior and your thoughts.

Here is Christ's powerful point. When the Holy Spirit indwells your heart, there is no such thing as Him "showing up." He is always there. You can't slip around behind His back and pull off a sin without Him seeing it. His presence in your heart is at once an all-seeing eye and an all-embracing love. What we used to do to our parents is not possible with God. God will never step out from behind a door with a "gotcha!" He is incapable of that.

He exists with equal awareness on both sides of the door! And that includes the door of your heart.

An old old book from the time of Christ called *The Manual of Discipline* — perhaps compiled by a group which John the Baptist belonged to — declares, "All the sons of justice tread in the ways of light" (III.20). The change that God brings to our lives is not a covering that He drapes around us; it is a transformation that He makes within us. A Christian is a different person in essence from when he was first born. His life has been invaded with the presence of God so that he no longer lives for himself, but for his intended purpose — to bring glory and honor to God.

A person who claims to be a Christian, but who still reeks with self-indulgence, has not been transformed. A person who claims to be a Christian, but who can slither and slide into any old behavior depending on where he is, still needs the transformation which salvation brings. A person who is only a Christian when he is around Christians is not yet a Christian.

It is a red-letter day in the life of any Christian when God can stop having to push him from behind and can begin compelling him from within. It is a joy to go forward, not because necessity is treading on our heels, but because we have Someone up ahead who is inspiring us forward.

It's a sentence that deserves a second look. A person who is only a Christian when he is around Christians is not yet a Christian.

3 A HOLY LIFE MEANS THAT WE HAVE STOPPED ASKING ABOUT MINIMUMS.

"For I tell you that unless your righteousness surpasses that of the Pharisees and the teachers of the law, you will certainly not enter the kingdom of heaven" (Matt. 5:20).

Al Michaels, emcee of Monday Night Football, said about one player, "I never saw him make a tackle first. He always ran around looking ferocious until someone else made the first hit, then he piled on top for the glory."

I still meet the question too often, "Joe, how much will I have to give up to live for God?" In a world of measured commitments, prenuptial agreements, and partial sacrifice, even a little can seem like a lot. But if the early disciples teach us anything, they insist that we must leave all. They left all — which wasn't much by our standards today.

Whatever you and I have to give up won't tally up much higher. Two millennia haven't increased the total very much. You will never in your life hear the testimony, "I'm so sorry I gave my life to Christ. I've regretted it almost every day I've lived. If only I hadn't followed Christ, my life would have been so much better."

> The true disciple of Christ has learned:
>
> . . . that to be called by Christ is a mission,
>
> . . . that to be bound to Christ is freedom,
>
> . . . that to die for Christ is life.

Ours is a culture of portable loyalties. Everybody and his brother will crusade for a cause — for a day. What we need are more people who will pay cash, throw away the receipt and never have a thought of going back.

If the sun and moon were as committed to their jobs as many are to their faith, we wouldn't know if it were a bright night or a dark day.

4 A HOLY LIFE FLOWS OUT OF A HEART OF PURE LOVE.

"But I tell you: Love your enemies and pray for those who persecute you, that you may be sons of your Father in heaven. He causes his sun to rise on the evil and the good, and sends rain on the righteous and the unrighteous" (Matt. 5:44-45).

God never wastes a consecrated life.

> A drop in the bucket
>   Is only a drop,
>   A minor and moist detail;
>   For a drop can't change
>   the color and taste
>   In a ten-quart watering pail.
>
> But if that drop
>   Has the color of love
>   And the taste of tears divine,
>   One drop dropped into the vessel of life
>   Can change the water to wine.
>
>   — Helen Kromer
>   In *Inspiring Quotations* by Wells[1]

The Christian life is nothing more or less than a gradual unveiling of God to the soul. All of us have glimpses of God. But the pure in heart have come to see Him most plainly. Architect Ralph Crom used to say that a church building should be stronger in structure and richer in materials the farther you go. When it is, it becomes truly symbolic of Christian character.

Holiness is simply the internalization of God's power and purity to such a degree that it becomes our chief inspiration and our highest drive. Thomas Á Kempis described the only way to reach that second level of living. "Make God," he said, "the supreme habit of your soul." The Christian faith is not a ball and chain to hang around your neck, but a soaring, stirring, happy thing.

By nature, love is jealous — not jealous in a possessive, controlling sense — jealous in its desire for the full loyalty of the one loved. On the other hand, a person who thoroughly loves someone is not out looking for another option. His vision is narrow, his heart focused, his admiration fixed.

If we love God with our whole heart, we will try to bend every behavior to show our total loyalty. As a husband, a father and a normal male, I have committed myself to the following list of behaviors to show God, my wife and children that I want to fully honor my marriage pledge. These are my Ten Commandments for Personal Purity.

TEN COMMANDMENTS FOR PERSONAL PURITY

- I will never watch TV while I am alone at home or in a hotel.
- I will never meet with another woman behind a closed door.
- I will open and close every day by reading my Bible.
- I will always alert my wife when physical temptation is high.
- I will first say "yes" to Christ before I say "no" to sin.
- I will shop more often at stores that sell less trash.
- I will call Christ as the co-inspector of all my thoughts.
- I will immediately turn from any media which arouses wrong thoughts.
- I will always keep in mind my final accounting in the presence of Christ.
- I will conduct myself exactly as I want my son to conduct himself someday.

I hope you have a list like that, a set of non-negotiables for your heart.

5 A HOLY LIFE STEERS CLEAR OF DELIBERATE DAILY SIN.

"Likewise every good tree bears good fruit, but a bad tree bears bad fruit. A good tree cannot bear bad fruit, and a bad tree cannot bear good fruit . . . by their fruit you will recognize them" (Matt. 7:17-20).

Damon Runyan, in a New York Times editorial, stuck a knife into the heart of the problem:

> It would help our world if ministers would occasionally stand up, haul off and slap the ears off evil. We point to every reason under the sun why our society is having so many problems, but let us point one more time and let us point plainly in the direction of sin.

Let me use an analogy which touches a nerve: abortion. We evangelicals have long argued that life starts at conception. We rail against those who argue that until the second or third trimester a life is not a life and that it can be aborted without any harm being done. We say — correctly — that life begins at conception and no amount of logic or selfishness can budge that law.

Let's use the same logic with sin. There is a growing number of Christians who laugh about their occasional sins. They all but brag that in our day it is impossible to live without sin, even deliberate sin. But tell me. At what point along the path of the mind does a desire become a sin. Does it really not matter too much until the desire is two months old? Or three? Why don't we just forget about trying to resist sin? After all, it's not really dangerous until it comes to maturity. As long as it's in the mind, it does no harm.

Does life begin at conception? Does sin begin at the point of desire? If we say that abortion is abortion at the point of conception and that it is wrong to abort after that, why don't we come down with equal vigor on the fact that sin is sin at the point of desire and allow God to help us before it starts? This business of sinning for a while, planning to stop before it goes too far, is a lot of hogwash. If God can come into our hearts and forgive sin after it starts, surely He can get there early enough to keep it from starting.

I tire of those who think we will get so holy we will lose touch with reality. Listen, the real saints of our world are more aware of their sins and shortcomings than the rash of sinners who assume they're holy. Let's get off the merry-go-round of Christian commitment where we are forever circling back and starting all over again. If we are quick to urge people to refrain from the kind of behavior which results in aborted babies, we should be equally quick to call God to our rescue before we engage in any kind of inward choices that lead to sin. If you lust after mountains and beaches, you have already committed vacation in your heart.

Let's not keep excusing what God can prevent. God can help us avoid deliberate sin. If He can't, our salvation is faulty and we need a better brand. Jesus did not die to help us win the sin battle 51% of the time; He died to help us quit the sinning business. I am weary of the line, "Well, there's so much confusion on how to state holiness, that it must not be biblical. If God really meant us to have it, He would have made it clearer."

But please tell me this. What if we treated worship the same way? There are people who love choruses on Sunday morning and others who think hymns are on the same plain of revelation as the Scriptures. There are some who want the rafters to shake from shouting and others who think they should smell from incense. But just because we see every way under the sun for coming to God, do we throw out worship as unscriptural? Hardly. We celebrate the diverse ways in which God lets us climb His holy hill.

Watch the cars drive down your street. There is every brand and breed you can think of — on the outside. But underneath they all have an engine and a steering mechanism and a gear to turn the wheels. The externals of how we move toward holiness are far less important than how we are relating to God deep in our hearts. Frankly, I don't want an '87 car if I can help it. (Right now, I can't!) Oh, I'll take the engines they made back then. But I want the outside to be a bit more modern.

This whole mindset of dabbling around in sin every other hour is not a truth from the Bible, but a lie from the Liar. I grant that Christians occasionally fall into sin because of too close an association with evil or because of human fatigue. But to make a habit out of it under the excuse that it can't be helped is to mock God. We need to ask ourselves, "Do I really want to quit sin or do I just want to keep sinning and bend the Bible data so it smiles on my sinfulness?" If God can't help us cease sinning, then how in the world can He really forgive it? If He's not powerful enough to keep it from starting, what makes us think He is powerful enough to halt it once it's in motion?

> If we have to sin every day, what's the use of worship?
>
> If we have to sin every day, why not take a rain check on the faith until we get within a few steps of death and then take care of it in one closing prayer?
>
> If we have to sin every day, how is a Christian different from a sinner?
>
> If we have to sin every day, then what, for instance, does salvation do for us?

In his book *He Sent Leanness*, David Head includes what should be called "The Manifesto of Shallow Living." He shapes it in the form of a prayer:

> Most benevolent and easy going Father, we have occasionally been guilty of errors in judgment. We have lived under the deprivations of heredity and the disadvantages of environment. We have done the best we could do in the circumstances and have been careful not to ignore common standards of decency. We are glad to know that we are fairly normal.
>
> Do please, O Lord, deal lightly with our infrequent lapses. Be your own sweet self with those who admit that they are not perfect according to your unlimited tolerance which we have a right to expect from you. And grant, as the Great Indulgent Parent, that we may hereafter continue to live a harmless and happy life where the demands upon us shall be even less.[2]

A HOLY PERSON BUILDS EACH DAY SO THAT THE "LIFE STRUCTURE" WILL LAST FOREVER.

"Therefore everyone who hears these words of mine and puts them into practice is like a wise man who built his house on the rock" (Matt. 7:24).

It is appropriate that a Carpenter would close His sermon with an illustration from His own early career. He closes with a story about a construction project. He had lived 30 years, long enough to see a home constructed, fall into disrepair, then disuse, then crumble into the shifting sands as the winds and rain beat upon it. Jesus knew from experience that the dream of excellence is constructed from the details of commitment.

If you look at this closing parable carefully, you will see a very vital detail. The choice of where to build made all the difference. A lot of the later decisions made by the builders all traced back to the original choice of the site. One chose rock, the other sand. They might have lived within eyeshot of each other. They might even have been friends.

Rock and sand are usually not that far apart. Sand laps up around the rock, as close as a person sitting beside you in the pew.

In a local newspaper editorial, Columnist George Will said, "This country was born in a struggle to remove restraints imposed from without. Today it is struggling to achieve restraints arising from within." Too many people have aimed to follow themselves and they have set their sights too low. Whatever else you do in life, get as close to God as you can. Don't miss a bit of His blessing. "Holy" is a good word, because "holy" is God's word.

I had been a Christian for about a year when I began to sense a need for a deeper work of God in my life. I had known first faith; now I sensed a need for great faith. I especially needed help to overcome several habits that kept cropping up in my life. When I first knelt to ask Jesus into my life as Savior, I had asked Him to forgive me of my sins and He did. I had no doubts about that. But I couldn't seem to overcome several deeply-grooved habits that were still surfacing in my behavior. For example, I would still catch myself swearing at times. I didn't plan to, but I would get under pressure and let words fly from my lips that don't belong in the Christian vocabulary.

Plus, I was not consistent in my witness for Christ. When I got with the wrong group, I was too easily influenced into telling the wrong kind of jokes and thinking the wrong kinds of thoughts. I found myself confessing and falling, confessing and falling far too often. My own logic, even before I got to the Bible, told me that Jesus' death on the cross must surely be able to help me with more personal victory than I was enjoying. I had already discovered that God loves us with sacrifical love, so I began turning to Him in prayer for a greater level of spiritual consistency.

That was key. When people tell me they can't be truly holy, I always say this, "I won't argue with you a split second on that. But I encourage you to do this. Go inside your spirit and honestly answer this one question, 'Which way is your spirit leaning?' If you are genuinely leaning toward God with an openness to all of His presence and power, I don't have the slightest worry about you. But if you are leaning against any more of His empowering and cleansing, you are risking even your salvation."

Truth is, if you are leaning in God's direction, you are making progress.

In His time and way, He will come in to fill you with a greater level of His Spirit so that not just your behaviors, but your very motive, will be transformed and redirected to His will. That is no small work on God's part. But it all begins with you leaning firmly and clearly in His direction.

That night I went to church with my heart leaning as far toward God as I could let it lean. A man named Rev. Glenn Griffith preached on missions, which had nothing to do with my immediate need. When he asked for those who wanted to become missionaries to come forward, I went forward to ask for the infilling of the Spirit.

I have never had a call to missions and didn't get one that night. But I did have a major need in my spirit. I needed God to realign my own person around His glory and honor. I was leaning toward Him, but I needed for Him to take my surrendered spirit and bring it into harmony with His heart. I knelt there while somebody prayed for me to be a great missionary and asked God to make me a holy person. I can honestly say that it was a tremendous step upward in my walk with God. I found a new level of spiritual victory, a new power for witnessing, a new dynamic in my love for God.

Augustine crafted a classic, "May God bring us to a point where our will is so lost in God's will that we cannot tell the difference between the two."

When people say to me that a person can't live with a consistent desire to please God all the time I say, "baloney." That's the only normal way TO live. What kind of holiness would you have that wasn't entire? Why live for Christ if you plan to be a compartmental Christian? And if God can bring our will into closer alignment with His will by a major gift of grace, who in their right mind wouldn't want it?

Helmut Thielicke, a theologian and preacher, says, "How little people know who assume that holiness is dull. When one meets the real thing, it is irresistable. Living for God is not dull stagnation, but a soaring, stirring, happy thing."[3]

A little closer to home Dr. Lee Haines, in an article entitled, "Articulating and Living Christian Holiness in a Pluralistic World," concludes:

> . . . I talk about a second event, an intensifying event in the life of the Christian, involving surrender of the will and trust in Christ, and also involving the cleansing, filling, health-giving work of God in the person's life at that time. I preach that this step is so natural that unless the Spirit's work is resisted, He will lead every child of God by this point, whether the theology is understood or not, whether the terms are known or not.[4]

Is your will so lost in God's will that you can't tell the difference between the two? If you sense a gap between God's will for you and where you are presently, why not begin your prayer for God to close the gap even now?

Endnotes

[1]Albert M. Wells, Jr., ed., *Inspiring Quotations* (Nashville: Thomas Nelson, 1988), p. 95.
[2]David Head, *He Sent Leanness* (New York: Macmillan, 1959), p. 19.
[3]Ian Barclay, *Living and Enjoying the Fruit of the Spirit* (Chicago: Moody Press, 1979), p. 36.
[4]Lee Haines, "Articulating and Living Christian Holiness in a Pluralistic World" (Paper presented at the Nazarene/Wesleyan Theology Conference in Kansas City, MO, Feb. 27, 1972), p. 3.

Mind Movers

1 Holiness means different things to different people. How would you define it as you understand its use in the Bible? Are most Christians living holy lives, or is holiness an ideal for more mature saints?

2 When God calls us to be holy as He is holy, what does that mean?

3 If only holy people can live in heaven, what will happen to people who claim to be Christians but are not truly holy when they die?

4 Is holiness an option for Christians who want to go deeper with God? Is it really necessary for salvation?

5 Can a person be a Christian and at the same time not desire to be holy?

Ultimacy

9

Choices that Matter Most in the End

Chris Darden, one of the prosecutors in the O.J. Simpson criminal trial, pointed his finger at Mr. Simpson and spoke more truth than the media can manage: "Mr. Simpson, never forget it. There will be a final court and on that day, your accusers will be the two eyewitnesses to the crime — Ron Goldman and Nicole Brown."

Simpson snickered. But Darden made an eternal point. Of what use would it be to save your face and lose your soul? Why mortgage your future for a final fling of pleasure in the present?

When I polled 260 high school students on what they believed happened to people after death, the responses revealed a generation suffering from blurry vision. Their thoughts can be clustered into percentages:

34%	We will be absorbed into a sort of mass calmness.
23%	We will enter into a life of peace and light.
16%	We will go to be with God if we have been mostly good.
14%	We will cease to exist in any kind of personal way.
5%	We will be returned to earth to inhabit another body.
5%	We will go to either heaven or hell.
3%	We will live forever if we are good and be annihilated if we have not lived well.

Today, getting a person to think about consequences next week is a challenge; for eternity, a miracle. Evangelists who seek to move people by pointing to heaven and hell often find themselves preaching with the soft pedal down. The truth fails to land — at least land hard. Look at a few recent statements made right in church:

- I hope I can stay loyal to Christ for life. I'm not very good on staying committed to anything for long, but with Christianity, I want to try.

- I will try to teach a class, but I don't want to teach for more than a quarter. I need to be careful about taking on more long-term commitments.

- This marriage thing is scary. I know my grandparents stayed together all their lives, but it's a different day. I sure hope we can stick together for a long time.

- I sure would hate to go to hell. I don't know how long God will make it last, but 15 seconds would be 15 seconds too long.

In popular culture, commitment has been redefined from a "forever" value to a "whenever" value. "Till death do us part" has become "till boredom do us part." The one-word slogan is popping up on bib overalls, caps and tee shirts. It is symptomatic of the times: *"Whenever."*

We are involved with people holding the "Felix fallacy." Felix was the Roman leader who listened to Paul's testimony but delayed responding to Paul's Christ. His philosophy calls up sadness. Listen to this pathetic paragraph. "As Paul discoursed on righteousness, self-control and the judgment to come, Felix was afraid and said, 'That's enough for now! You may leave. When I find it convenient, I will send for you.'" (Acts 24:25 NIV)

But Jesus still states the truth in unequivocal terms. He never set His message by the windsock of His times.

When short men cast long shadows, you know the sun is setting.

Just because His hearers sorted through His teachings and tossed out what they didn't like didn't turn Him into an ear tickler. There were plenty in the audience that afternoon near Galilee who doubted the resurrection of the dead. In that day, too, He looked into the faces of people who assumed that eternity was a giant ball of soul dough.

But Jesus included the eternal in His message without the slightest hint of accommodating their view. If something is true, the size of the group that denies it is irrelevant. You don't shut down a radio station by turning off the knob. Covering a bent nail with white chocolate doesn't make it a pretzel. And bending the laws of God to fit our game doesn't alter a single thing.

People today are much more concerned about life *before* death than they are about life *after* death.

- "*Heaven*" is a five-star home.
- "*Salvation*" is a life of comfort and enough money to enjoy recreation every weekend.
- "*Contentment*" is having the latest gadgets from the techno journals.
- "*God*" is a sense of alignment with the energies of the universe.
- "*Eternal life*" is a body free of pain and one that can easily be healed by a trip to the doctor.

No one in all the Bible mentions our ultimate destinies of heaven and hell as often as Jesus. Sixteen times He allows the dreadful word "hell" to escape His lips.

In spite of the gaping chasm that separates heaven and hell, there are a number of features which they share in common.

1 BOTH ARE PERSONAL.

In the end, there are only two final moral sanctions: eternal life and eternal death. Emily Dickinson collects this truth and wraps it in poetry:

> *This world is not conclusion*
> *A sequel stands beyond*
> *Invisible as music*
> *Yet positive as sound.* [1]

Faith is like a toothbrush. Everybody needs one, but nobody shares one. Two people using one toothbrush dirties up the mouth of both. Share toothpaste? Yes. Share a toothbrush? No. We cannot have faith for another. We will stand before God one at a time, single file. The call to step forward will not be issued en masse. We often hear of the throngs and throngs of people who will stand before Christ at the last day. But don't let the crowd language throw you. You will not be standing in a crowd, half hidden behind your grandfather when Jesus calls your name. You will be standing uncamouflaged — a single, solitary soul before the Savior.

When your sentence is pronounced, there will be no chance to mistake its owner. The words will be as clearly yours as the thumbprint which you now carry on your hand.

2 BOTH ARE SENSORY.

With all the joking about heaven and hell that goes on around us, it is easy to fall into thinking that heaven and hell are not that different. Popular talk has so blurred the lines of distinction between them that people glibly say, "Oh, if I go to hell, at least I'll have good friends." They then turn right around and sneer heaven, "Boy, that will be boring, sitting in a rocking chair all day."

The signal that sticks is that heaven and hell are superficially different, but fundamentally similar. But just the opposite is actually true. They are as fundamentally different as any two realms of existence could be.

The one will mean ultimate comfort.
  The other unstopping pain.

The one an oasis for the soul.
  The other an eternal mirage.

The one a life of fellowship with God.
  The other a life of bitterness toward Satan.

The one a haven of rest.
  The other a caldron of hate.

Our senses will be fully alive. Some will embrace the joys of heaven in a feast of the soul. Others will endure the agonies of hell in a famine of death.

One man quipped, "Make your reservations for eternity now, 'smoking' or 'non-smoking.'" Frankly, it's not funny.

3 BOTH ARE ENDURING.

We have an eternal internal. Most of our lifetimes will not be spent on earth. No analogy is perfect, but imagine the string that tethers the kite to your hand. Compared to eternity, this life is only the four or five inches you hold in your hand. All the rest of the string, as far as the eye can see, represents the vast future world.

If you took a thimble down to the ocean and began the process of emptying the waters of the seas into some imaginary container on another planet, the end of your errand would only be the beginning of eternity.

If you could pick just one leaf at a time from all the trees on earth and place them in infinite rows of floral designs, your creative artwork would last millions of years and still not reach the rain forests. And eternity would have only begun.

> *Eternity is the next number after infinity.*
> *Eternity is the last thought that God will ever think.*
> *Eternity makes light years look like seconds.*
> *Eternity is the timepiece on God's arm.*
> *Eternity is the circle that begins as it ends.*

When you are tempted to overfocus on this life, go out and look up into the night sky and remember that you are merely looking at God's front yard.

Please don't call what you are seeing "the universe." We've only ventured to the first satellite of our own world. It's hardly time for us to lay claim to understanding the stretches of the universe. But even then, we understand it about as well as we do eternity.

4. BOTH ARE PURPOSEFUL.

God always follows through on His word. Every part of His plan has a purpose. Heaven and hell have a purpose. They are the necessary destinies of two types of lifestyles.

No one ever went to heaven whose heart was not there before. It is the power of the treasure to draw the heart after it. It is a simple law of life that where your treasure is, there your pleasure is.

G. B. Caird said:

> The man who habitually puts his trust in God and tries to follow in the steps of Jesus Christ will become the sort of person who would be at home in the presence of God. The man who laughs at the gospel, breaks all the rules, and throws away his life in unrepentent waste, will be the sort of person who would be more seriously out of place in heaven than a tone-deaf man in a roomful of musicians.[2]

That is why a person who has lived a life of sinful pleasure would be ill-at-ease in heaven. Heaven would make him as uncomfortable as a thief at a party of prosecutors. Chrysostom once said, "What a folly to leave your treasures in the place from which you are going away, instead of sending them before you to where you are going."

We will have a clear sense of why we are in heaven. We will know it is not based on how good we were. And wouldn't you just hate it if people could earn their way to heaven and you would have to spend eternity listening to all the bragging?

The purpose of hell will be to continue the self-indulgence of this life — with equal hollowness at the end of the binge. Hell will be indulgence in self with all the joy of swimming in an inch-deep pool.

It is a law of life that for every action there is an equal and opposite reaction. Since that is true, what does sin deserve? If sin is a slap in the face of God, then who gets slapped in return? How foolish for us to slap God in the face and assume that He will just laugh it off and go His way. In the end, our whole life will be met with either a slap or a caress, either "Well done" or

"Get out." For that reason, our whole life should be a Lenten Season, preparing us for the Sabbath of our death and the Easter of our Resurrection.

The global culture is dragging the mindset of the masses toward a global faith, a tangled skein of teachings that have neither coherence nor worth, a kind of ecclesiastical osmosis which allows for both leakage and absorption.

The Christian worldview is calling us to remember the crisis of the ultimate, the dividing line between the world of time and the world of eternity. It reminds us of the slim number of days we have here in our audition on earth to prepare to meet our God.

5 BOTH ARE CHOICES.

Hell is a choice.

Heaven is a choice.

There is no land-based route to heaven. Nor to hell. You have to decide which ticket you will hold at the end. And the destiny is strictly up to you.

The whole argument that God is unfair to send anybody to hell is just so much boxing with the breeze. Not one verse in all the Bible reads, "So God sent the man to hell in spite of all the man could do to head in the other direction." On the other hand, there are thousands of verses which show God urging a person to choose heaven.

William Barclay has said:

> A man owes himself and everything else to Jesus Christ; and there is nothing that a man can give to Christ in place of his life. It is quite possible for a man to try to give his money to Christ, and yet to withhold his life. It is still more possible for a man to give lipservice to Christ, and to withhold his life. Many a person gives his weekly freewill offering to the Church, but does not go to Church; obviously that does not satisfy the demands of Church membership. The only possible gift to the Church is ourselves; and the only possible gift to Christ is our whole life. There is no substitute for it, and nothing less will do.[3]

Reality In A Hamburger

The family in the restaurant was an ordinary family — a dad, a mom, and an eleven-year-old boy. The waitress took the orders.

"And what would you like, ma'am?" she began.

"I'll have the roast beef, green beans, corn and a tossed salad," the mother replied.

The waitress turned to the father. He ordered a balanced meal, similar to his wife's. The waitress then turned to the boy.

"And what would you like, sonny?"

"A hamburger and french fries," he began. Both parents barked at once.

"You will not! You're going to stop eating that junk food. Pick something healthy or we'll have to pick for you!" they declared.

The waitress waited for them to finish.

"And what would you like on your hamburger, sonny?" she continued.

"Tomato and mayonnaise," he said, grinning. "And lots of it."

Without another word the waitress whirled around and disappeared through the swinging metal doors into the kitchen. The little boy turned slowly toward his parents.

"You know what? That lady thinks I'm real!"

So does God. God will let you choose fast food, or no food, or bland food — your choice. And it's a profound choice. This notion that any old road will do because they all reach the top is going to send a lot of people to a sad eternity. If sincerity saves us, we don't need a Bible — we just need a good believing heart.

But sincerity is not helpful if your ladder is propped against the wrong wall. My wife was sincere as a child when she thought that AM and FM meant "American Music" and "Foreign Music," but that didn't make her right. Plus, it bothered her a bit that she liked "foreign music" better. There is a body of truth which God has revealed and we do well to train our minds to think God's thoughts.

The "crossover craze" has gone to seed. A great many who ought to know better are touting the New Age as the hot rage. Jesus Himself said that many false "christs" would arise, but He begged us not to follow them. Like so many pied pipers, they are leading our children outside the shelter of our values and steering them down a slippery trail.

BOTH ARE FINAL.

Change a word or two and you could hang this sign from an airman's school over the entrance way to eternity:

> *"Remember your parachute.*
> *If you need it and don't have it,*
> *you will never need it again."*

One man's point made sense. He sat in his lounge chair and listened respectfully as the pastor invited him to church. Not one ounce of concern showed on his face.

"But, Pastor, I just don't think I need the church," he said. "My wife and daughter enjoy coming. They both love me very much. If I were in any real danger, I figure they would tell me."

In our culture where tolerance is king, the exclusive claims of the gospel are jeered. Even Christians are leaning more and more to a mindset that holds that while Christianity is still effective, other religions can also help others to God. That is a dangerous mental step. Tolerance will be a poor excuse when we stand before Christ and He asks, "Did you tell others about the way to heaven?"

> *Is it being elitist and intolerant if a medical doctor*
> *travels to another country and administers*
> *care to the poor?*
>
> *Is it elitist and intolerant if a policeman*
> *runs to the aid of a man who is being robbed?*
>
> *Is it elitist and intolerant if a neighbor*
> *calls the emergency number if a house is*
> *burning down?*

Then why should it be considered elitist and intolerant if one person tells another how to save his eternal soul? If people are lost without Christ and on their way to a sad future, who in their right minds wouldn't get their attention and tell them to turn around? If you are turning a person from the error of his ways, don't let anyone make you think you are revisiting the Spanish Inquisition. You are simply telling them the truth.

John Patton, Archbishop of Canterbury, gave John Wesley sound advice: "Do not spend your time and strength in contending for or against things that are of a disputable nature. Spend your time testifying against open notorious vices and in promoting real, essential holiness."

Recently I preached on heaven and hell in a morning service and met this comment from a young father at the door. "I'm glad you mentioned that heaven and hell stuff, pastor. I had almost forgotten it was in the Bible. You don't hear much about it anymore."

Dan Brummit, whose office sits just across the street from a busy intersection, once said, "If I get killed crossing that intersection, just put on my tombstone, 'He died from looking in the wrong direction.'"

In whatever direction you are looking, be sure you turn from time to time to remind yourself that eternity is out in front of you. 2 Corinthians 5:10 says, "For we must all appear before the judgment seat of Christ, that each one may receive what is due him for the things done while in the body, whether good or bad" (NIV).

I attended the funeral of Evangelist Jimmy Lentz. In the eulogy, Dr. David Watson included this line, "When Brother Jimmy came to cross the Jordan River he was happy because his father owned the property on both sides of the river."

Endnotes

[1]Emily Dickinson, *The Manuscript Books of Emily Dickinson,* ed. R.W. Franklin, Vol. 1 (Cambridge: Harvard University Press, 1981), p. 396.

[2]G. B. Caird, *The Truth of the Gospel* (London: Oxford University Press, 1950), p. 126.

[3]William Barclay, *The Gospel of Matthew, Volume 2* (Philadelphia: The Westminster Press, 1958), p. 170.

Mind Movers

1 Have heaven and hell lost their power to influence people toward God today? Explain your thinking.

2 Have people stopped thinking very much about heaven and hell?

3 Is heaven a real place with gold streets or is that just a metaphor to suggest the beauty of heaven? Is hell actually a place of fire or is that just a metaphor to suggest the awful pain of being separated from Christ?

4 If hell is really real, why aren't people out evangelizing every person they can find to keep them from going there?

5 Do you believe that heaven has lost some of its draw because people are too comfortable in this life? Are you personally drawn to heaven as a place of excitement and beauty?

6 What has caused people to lose a sense of urgency about preparing for the world to come?

Succession

10

Shining Your Flashlight Behind You

At least Bob Cosgrove was honest. For more than ten years he had been a member of my church. He had served the usual ascending string of committees, right up to the Local Board. Not one thing in his life raised even the slightest hint of suspicion that anything was wrong. His wife never suspected it. His children ran with the church youth. His tithe hit the plate on the first Sunday. Many pastors would give two or three lesser players in a good swap. But Bob knew better. His testimony told his heart:

> For these ten years I have been committing one of the most deadly sins ever to grip a church. I have been committing the sin of apathy. I have done the right things — at the minimum level. I have given to the right causes — at the minimum level. I have served on our board — at a minimal level.

But lately I've been struggling with myself. I have no known outward sins in my life. I am a good father, a decent husband. But I have no passion for God. And I am watching my children grow up with the same mediocre spirit. They do the right things, run with the right people and stand out in the youth group, but I can tell they are not ablaze for God.

And if they are ever going to give their max to the Master, their father is going to have to set the pace. I want to go on record before this body this morning and say, "Bob Cosgrove is committing himself to a new level of Christian living. I want to live with a passion for God. I want to burn for God. I want my wife and children to see a new dad, a new husband, a new spiritual leader in our home."

As Bob sat down, his eyes filling with tears, the congregation broke into spontaneous applause. In the months that followed, Bob Cosgrove became a firebrand for God. The fire that burned in his life sent renewal sweeping through the entire church.

Let's not be fancy and complicate commitment out of existence. You and I both know that if God can break through the spirit of Bob Cosgrove — one ordinary man — and spark a contagion in the whole body, He can do it all over again. If just one person in every church would resolve to go deeper with God and make it known in testimony and in his life, we could chuck our stash of methods and just ride the holy wave.

> *The person will never go far for God who does not first go deep with God.*

You can be sure that the Man standing by the Sea of Galilee in the gentle breeze was doing anything but calling for a gentle breeze. The last thing on His mind was how to squeeze all the testimonies and prayers and the sermon into one hour so the chicken wouldn't scorch in the oven. Baloney on the chicken!

If they needed lunch, He could find that boy with the fish and chips. Jesus wasn't up there calling for a calm, don't-rock-the-boat friendship with the world. His sermon called for such pervasive holiness that it caused His followers to go out and capsize the world. Hardly your harmless homily!

124

At intervals in His sermon, He zeroed in on what that zeal for God would look like — zeal that would inspire a brand new generation to want some of it for themselves. He knew that great movements of God are never gotten by dialogue, but by proclamation. People who move people are the most devoted people in the world.

Focus on the Master as He speaks to the characteristics which make others want to follow our God.

1 LIVE SO THAT PEOPLE SEE NOT HYPOCRISY, BUT A RADICAL SINCERITY.

In Matt. 6:5 Jesus aims an arrow: Don't be a hypocrite. People in our generation want to see a clean life, not one that claims to be clean but inwardly is as dirty as a dumpster. They want to see a sparkling clear spirit that refreshes on impact, one that reminds us again that purity is not passé, that holiness is still the living standard, that a sterling pure love for God is possible in this lust-filled world.

I'm tired of the crowd that claims you need to sin a little every day in order to be accepted by the world. Whoever said we needed the world's acceptance? Why in the world would we want the approval of a culture that doesn't know purity from a hole in the ground? If you have to keep sinning to help sinners, they why didn't Jesus sin? He refused to sin and He helped out quite a bit. And right in this very sermon He calls us to be holy even as He is holy.

Give us purity of heart, integrity of life, zeal of will. Let us cry out against sin and let our loudest cry be our own holy lives. Let us show others that a person can live fully and finally for God; that we don't need to tamper around with sin in order to save the sinner; that purity must not be sacrificed to bring others to salvation.

Sydney Carter folds this truth in four living lines:

> *The Living Truth is what I long to see*
> *I cannot lean on what I used to be*
> *So shut the Bible and show me how*
> *The Christ you talk about is living now.*[1]

As the song puts it, "May all who come behind us find us faithful." Let's move from being counted *in* to being counted *on*.

In Jim Elliot's immortal words, "God makes his ministers a flame of fire. Am I ignitable? God deliver me from the dread asbestos of other things. Saturate me with the oil of the Spirit that I may be aflame."

Be real. Burn for God. Praise Him openly. Get on board. Quit straddling the lines. Go all out. Consecrate everything. Hold nothing back. Crave the purity where God lives. Be holy.

LIVE SO THAT PEOPLE SEE NOT SELF-IMPORTANCE, BUT HUMILITY.

When I was a child, I was impressed with the prodigious number of songs in our hymnal by a man named "Anonymous." I wish there were more Anonymous people who didn't need their face on Rushmore to do more.

Self-righteousness has never been popular. It is even less so in a society that has been inoculated against religion by a handful of shysters who mistake their orbit for God's. People who are trying to save themselves are pioneering in something already discovered. People who exalt themselves have the wrong person doing the lifting. In Revelation 3:14-20, Jesus rebukes the Laodiceans for lukewarmness. Lukewarmness is caused by self-sufficiency. The testimony of the Laodicean Church — "I . . . have need of nothing" (NASB) — was both premature and immature.

In the Incarnation, God tipped His hand. He emptied Himself and became obedient unto death, even death on a cross. If Christ humbled Himself and became obedient unto death, we need to ditto the deed. Always be seeking the lower place where Christ spends most of His time.

LIVE SO THAT PEOPLE SEE NOT MEDIOCRITY, BUT A FLAMING PASSION FOR GOD.

Matthew 6:2 says: "So when you give to the needy, do not announce it with trumpets, as the hypocrites do in the synagogues and on the streets, to be honored by men. I tell you the truth, they have received their reward in full" (NIV).

Commitment is a decision wrapped in a passion. John Chrysostom, the golden-tongued pastor of the fourth century, has said that Hannah wept many tears praying for one son but we yawn praying for a whole kingdom. A Christian never falls asleep in the fire, but he will likely grow drowsy in the sunshine.

A man who looked to be in his mid-twenties once gave this testimony, a plea for renewal: "I am part of a generation here in our church that has never seen a real renewal. We've heard about it, but we've never witnessed God's cleansing presence sweeping across this church. I urge you as older adults to not miss an opportunity to introduce this younger generation to the power of God."

Every generation deserves to see at least one real revival in its lifetime. Just like the Pharaoh who arose not knowing Joseph, so a new generation stands all about us, watching, yearning, needing a surging demonstration of the power of God. The young people in our churches need to see a revival, want to see a revival. They aren't sitting behind us in the pews and hoping we don't get too radical about this Christian thing. They crave an outbreak of God, a surging spirit of renewal which causes us to do something that's not in the bulletin.

Throughout Denmark you can see a great number of memorial parks and monuments for those who fell to Nazi terror. The Freedom Museum in Churchill Park in downtown Copenhagen has a memorial urn inscribed with these words from Otto Glested:

> You passing through the hall
> Stop here and think a moment
> Of those who in their sacrifice
> Gave us this reward
> And go your way
> But remember yours is the choice
> To waste their blood
> Or honor it in the flow of life.[2]

Never reduce the adventure of faith to a routine. Never allow your blaze for God to flicker down to the size of a match.

4 LIVE SO THAT PEOPLE SEE NOT HOARDING, BUT SHARING.

Matthew 6:19-24 is a whole sermon on sharing. Giving alms is the natural and most obvious external work of righteousness. Calvin Coolidge once observed that "No one has ever been honored for what he received. The only people we honor are those who give."[3]

When Jesus told the crowd not to let their money rust, He was serious. In those days, people didn't store coins in the bank; they buried them in the ground. The chemicals in the soil often corroded the money and made it worthless. George MacDonald in the book *Discovering the Character of God* asks, "Did Jesus ever put anything in his pockets?"

One of the most beautiful statements about the spirit of giving occurred in a church in Alabama. One Sunday morning, the tellers gathered the offering and found this note attached to the offering envelope, "I give ten dollars and myself, Mary I. McClellan, to God today."

> There are:
> - people who need others to survive.
> - people who can survive by themselves, but barely.
> - people who thrive and have something to spare.

5 LIVE SO THAT PEOPLE SEE NOT WORRY, BUT TRUST. (Matt. 6:25-34)

In Matthew 10:29, Jesus tells of two sparrows being sold for a penny. In Luke 26, He talks about five sparrows being sold for two pennies. A quick add on the math shows that if you buy four sparrows, the vendor will throw in a fifth sparrow for free.

The point Jesus makes is this: If God cares for worthless sparrows which are so cheap that you get a free one for buying two pennies worth, how much more can we trust Him? If He sees every sparrow that falls to the ground and counts them as carefully as He does the hairs of our heads, why can't we trust Him?

One man said, "I have to worry. I come from a long line of distinguished worriers." Not true. You can break the cycle. Worrying is dishonoring to God. It means we don't trust Him to plan our path and work His plan.

Philippians 4:6 reads, "Do not be anxious about anything, but in everything, by prayer and petition, with thanksgiving, present your requests to God" (NIV).

6 LIVE SO THAT PEOPLE SEE NOT A CRITICAL, BUT A LOVING SPIRIT.

Have you heard these lines?

> *I'm not stubborn, just firm in sticking to my principles.*
>
> *I'm not selfish, just don't believe in spoiling people.*
>
> *I'm not stingy, just know the value of a dollar.*
>
> *I'm not uncharitable, just happy to believe that truth is truth.*

You don't use sandpaper to clean your face. Why do you think it will be all that helpful to clean a spirit?

In *You Set My Spirit Free*, John of the Cross prays this prayer:

> *My Father, thank you that you want to set me free from a position I am not equipped to hold — that of judge. Thank you for opening my eyes to the truth that when I step into the role of judge at all, secret pride comes in and love goes out.*
>
> *Today, I will hold a "fast" on criticalness. Help me to act and speak only out of compassion, and to leave the judging and the outcome to you.*[4]

7 LIVE SO THAT PEOPLE SEE NOT PRIDE, BUT A HUMBLE SPIRIT.

Pride is not just a flaw on the surface of our lives, it is a tear in our hearts. C. S. Lewis writes, "Pride leads to every other vice; it is the complete anti-God state of mind. Pride is spiritual disease eating up the very possibility of love, or contentment or even of common sense."[5]

The "Parable Vase"

A bright red vase sits on the windowsill over the top of the rolltop desk that holds my computer. I did not buy the vase, and I have no idea of its market value. But I know this. It will never be on the twenty-five-cent table in our annual garage sale.

I received it from a couple named Andrew and Bernice Padgett, one of the most godly couples a young minister could ever meet. They were hard workers, pastors, and people who loved people with a surging spill-over kind of love. When Mrs. Padgett spoke to us at children's camp, I thought she was kidding when she told of taking drunkards into her home for the week. In my opinion, the Padgetts were right alongside God when it came to caring for the widows, the orphans and the children. I had never heard of someone loving the outcasts and the downcasts like that.

That's why this vase staggers me. One night after I had preached in a service, they asked for a moment to share. Andrew and Bernice stood there before the congregation and told how God had used my meager testimony to encourage them in their work. I honestly could not get the paradigm to flip over. They had been my own model of godliness for so many years that I simply could not reconcile their testimony with my own perception of myself.

The red vase is my parable of true humility. The very couple that epitomized humility giving a vase to a young preacher was just one more sign that they were as humble as they seemed. Not only were they God's servants, they could pass the credit for their work along to others who had done next to nothing to help them!

Augustine called humility the cheapest and yet best ornament of religion. Perhaps you have a vase in your home. Or some other kind of reminder of someone who has been a noble example of the holy love of God. Perhaps you glance at that symbol every now and then to remind yourself that you are not alone. That others have lived the life of commitment long before you ever set out to do it. That others have blazed the trail of full devotion so that your own steps can be more sure.

Endnotes

[1]Dick Innis, *I Hate Witnessing* (Ventura, CA: Regal Books, 1985), p. 42.
[2]Beatrice Levin, "The Freedom Museum," *Military History* (June 1994):77.
[3]Albert M. Wells, Jr., ed., *Inspiring Quotations,* p. 178.
[4]John of the Cross, *You Set My Spirit Free* (Minneapolis: Bethany House, 1994), p. 64.
[5]C. S. Lewis, *Christian Behavior* (New York: Macmillan, 1943), p. 45.

Mind Movers

1 In the end, every person is remembered for one great thing. Abraham for his faith, Job for his patience, Jesus for His salvation. If you could pre-plan how people would remember you, what would you have them say?

2 The legacy we leave is largely determined by the interests and causes to which we devote our time. Look over the following vital causes. What can a believer do to ensure that none of them gets overlooked in his busy life?

   A. Biblical values

   B. Family unity

   C. Inner peace

   D. Personal balance

   E. Purity of heart and life

   F. Stewardship of time and resources

   G. Cultivating wholesome relationships

   H. Preparing for eternity

3 Often the impression we make on family and friends is different from the one we want to make. What things can cause this discrepancy? What can a person do to close the gap between "intended impressions" and "actual impressions"?

4 When a culture is in moral decline, what can a person do to counter the moral freefall? Does the responsibility of Christians shift when society becomes increasingly hostile to their cause? Is social resistance harmful or helpful to the Christian cause? Support your view.

Keeping our Commitments in Balance

Conclusion

We live in a time when it's trendy to treat all faiths as valid, to believe that all roads lead to God. But Christianity never has and never will permit any rivals. In a day when diversity is deified and tolerance of anything and everything except Christianity is chic and stylish, Christianity stands alone, refusing to let the death of Jesus be just one more solution among the solutions.

I am fully aware that there are more than 1200 cults claiming to have the inside track on biblical truth. They line up to sneer at and label the rest of us as deceived and damned. I regret that, but I'm not going to lose my balance for a bunch of misguided fanatics. The truth is, Christianity is such a grand truth that it couldn't help but spawn a crowd of counterfeits. Jesus said it would happen. But I can't hang my head because a few people can't handle the power of God. Vance Havner used to say, "Where there's holy fire, there's bound to be wild fire, but, O God, give us fire."

People in our enlightened age wonder how a thinking person can swallow all the fantastic stories in the Bible — stories about ax heads that float and donkeys that talk and people who rise from the dead. To a rationalistic mind, they are the far-fetched fantasies of a fanatical few. But nobody in his right mind ever claimed that reason was the answer to everything. If we had faith enough to figure God out, we wouldn't need Him. So far I haven't found anybody who can sort out the facts, much less explain the mysteries which lie behind them. So I'm keeping faith with a God who has done the most for me in that direction.

I easily admit that I haven't figured out the answers to everything. I still have about as many questions as I do answers. But as I grow older there is one answer that I parade with increasing confidence. In my mind I have ventured down a thousand roads and imagined what life would be like if I lived it a hundred other ways. And always, when I return and start comparing my road with the one I just traveled in my mind, I am more sure than ever that Jesus is the answer. That the Man standing on the sloping mountain that afternoon near the Sea of Galilee is the key to life. He doesn't answer every question; He IS the answer to every question.

So please forgive me if I seemed obsessed with Jesus. It's true. So far I've met nothing that even comes close. And it's not just an occasional trek to a spiritual oasis. It's an everyday matter of the heart. It is a decision around which I have gathered my entire life.

You and I will involve ourselves in a wide range of activities which take our time and require the expenditure of precious energy. Most of them will involve work and play, friends and family, faith and values, shelter and protection, food and life. Those are the cardinal points of any balanced lifestyle.

The temptation of our time is to neglect one or more of the above in order to pursue another. It is the hallmark of our day that people will often let faith and values be the first to go. Eugene Peterson, author of *The Message*, assesses the spirit of the age.

> Religion in our time has been captured by the tourist mindset. Religion is understood as a visit to an attractive site to be made when we have adequate leisure. For some it is a weekly jaunt to church. For others, occasional visits to special services. Some, with a bent for religious entertainment and sacred diversions, plan their lives around special events like retreats, rallies and conferences. We go to see a new personality, to hear a new truth, to get a new experience, and so, somehow, expand our otherwise humdrum lives.

> The religious life is defined as the latest and the newest: Zen, faith-healing, human potential, parapsychology, successful living, choreography in the chancel, Armageddon. We'll try anything — until something else comes along.[1]

But for the Christian who wants to live in balance and total harmony with God, there is a higher way, a holier way. By building our lives daily on the Word and will of God, by spending regular time in His company, by sharing the good news with those around us, we can find the most fulfilling life one can live in this world. God honors the balanced life with the greatest peace.

Pastor Ray Barnwell calls it the "lego principle." The "lego principle" states that one circle is OK, two is better, but four will make for great stability. When we strike the proper balance in our range of commitments, the structure of our Christian life will rise to ever increasing heights.

In order to keep your balance, you will want to . . .
> . . . keep regular visits with your God-chosen priorities.
> . . . always be shoveling to greater depths in your shallowlands.
> . . . regularly take a day to back away.
> . . . respond to the very first signs of wobble.
> . . . cooperate and not fight with your "schedule."

You sometimes hear the line that people in Jesus' day could be more committed because, after all, life was much simpler. It was easier for them to find and focus on faith.

When I was a little boy, I remember those nights when my Dad and Mom would take my brother Dan and me down to the old pond below our house to see the bullfrogs. We would be sitting on the front porch sharing an evening of moon and stars and a "symphony" as only a clear country night can strike up: crickets and tree frogs taking the lead, with the beetles buzzing in harmony and moths dancing and fluttering around the porch light.

Then Dad would read my mind. "Let's walk down to the pond," he'd say and I was off for the giant yellow flashlight that hung on a nail in the back porch. I didn't know for sure, but as a boy I guessed that if there were people on the moon, they could see that flashlight if we stood real tall on our front porch and shined it in their direction.

There wasn't any clear trail down to the pond, just lots of blackberry vines and sedge bushes and fescue to trip or snag a little boy if he wasn't careful. But there was one big help. As Dad walked along in front of us, knocking down the bigger weeds and blazing a new path to the pond, he did one more thing that will always stand out in my mind. Every few steps he would turn around and shine the flashlight behind him. There we were: my little brother Dan, then me, then Mother bringing up the rear guard. And all of us would catch up to Dad by walking in the beam of the light.

I'm still walking in the light — not the light of a flashlight now, but the light of a thousand lives who have gone before. As I look out ahead of me, it's not dark at all. The path is as a shining light leading more and more into perfect day. And there out in front of them all walks the Savior. No wonder they called Him the Light of the world.

Endnote

[1]Eugene Peterson, *A Long Obedience in the Same Direction,* p. 12.

Mind Movers

1 What are the results to the church and to the Kingdom of God if Christians allow themselves to get out of balance in their commitments?

2 What are some criteria by which we might determine if a person is living a balanced Christian life?

3 How does God reveal Himself to be a God of balance? What can we observe in God's character that might teach us how to be better balanced in our own lives?

4 Why do cults often see such rapid allegiance to their cause, while the Christian faith struggles from a lack of deep commitment from its followers?

5 Can a Christian family regularly put ballgames before church attendance and still maintain balance in their family's Christian walk?

6 Think of a Christian person you believe demonstrates superior personal balance in his or her life. What features of this life would you like to see in your own?

Index

10 Laws of Commitment from the Sermon on the Mount